"In the midst of turmo  th
of fresh air."

ıvorite

"Vironika Tugaleva has written a vulnerable, relatable book with the potential to change lives. Infused with timeless wisdom and her personal experiences on the path from self-loathing to self-love, *The Love Mindset* offers hope, insight, and inspiration for healing and thriving. It's profound, yet accessible—a must-read for anyone who feels alone, ashamed, or love-deprived."

–Lori Deschene, founder of tinybuddha.com & author of
Tiny Buddha's 365 Tiny Love Challenges

"An authentic, brave and beautiful guide to a more loving self and a more loving world. A great gift of words for anyone searching for the sacred place of self-acceptance, self-understanding and self-love."

–Howard Falco, spiritual teacher and author of *I AM: The Power of Discovering Who You Really Are*

"If I had two words to describe *The Love Mindset*, they would be: fresh and powerful. This is because when I read it, something grabbed hold of me like it was the first time I'd seen a book in 5 years!"

–Reuben Lowe, *Mindful Creation*

THE LOVE MINDSET

An Unconventional Guide to Healing and Happiness

VIRONIKA TUGALEVA

Soulux Press

A publication of SOULUX PRESS.

To connect with the author, visit www.vironika.org

LIBRARY AND ARCHIVES CANADA CATALOGUING IN PUBLICATION DATA

Tugaleva, Vironika, 1988-, author

The love mindset : an unconventional guide to healing and happiness/ Vironika Tugaleva.

Issued in print and electronic formats.

ISBN 978-0-9920468-0-4 (pbk.).-- ISBN 978-0-9920468-2-8 (mobi).-- ISBN 978-0-9920468-1-1 (epub)

1. Self-acceptance. 2. Love--Religious aspects. I. Title.

BF575.S37T83 2013

158.1   C2013-905195-3

                                   C2013-905196-1

For Jamie

Love is the keynote of the universe –
The theme, the melody

Henry Abbey

CONTENTS

PREFACE

If someone would have told me several years ago that I would be writing a book about love, more so a spiritual one, I would have taken it as a joke. The message in *The Love Mindset* is not one that has arisen out of some religious conditioning, nor out of a lifetime pursuit in some discipline.

The pages of this book contain lessons about love from the fruit of my personal transformation that occurred after years of cynicism, self-loathing, and isolation. I have learned about love like our ancestors—as nomadic creatures—once learned about agriculture. I have found abundance simply through a lifetime of hunger and, now, if you would kindly invite me into your heart and mind, I would like to share with you what I have found to be, perhaps, the most important thing that any person can learn.

For most of my life, there were only a handful of things I had under control. I excelled at school, I had a way with words, and I knew how to convince people I was right. I spent my time talking about things as if I knew something about them, while slowly poisoning myself with anything I could get my hands on. The more it hurt, the more control I felt I had. I was spiralling blindly, armed with the power of shame-fuelled judgment and an arsenal of memories that I packaged conveniently into a "story." All in all, I was a master of self-destruction, arrogance, and playing victim. When it came to love, I always fell short.

Like most 21st century women, I spent most of my life hating my body. I desperately wanted to be beautiful and hated myself because I thought I wasn't. As an adult, I spent most of my hard-earned dollars removing, covering, altering, augmenting, decreasing, increasing, extending, and reducing. I cycled in and out of eating disorders for close to 10 years. When it wasn't food, it was some other self-altering obsession. I lived in a constant, steady state of complete self-rejection. My overriding goal was to be someone I wasn't. I wasn't sure who exactly I wanted to be, but certainly not myself.

I changed my hair, my face, my body. I tried to turn myself into someone other people would respond to with awe or envy. I wanted women to want to be me and men to want to be with me. I wanted to be desired and admired. I spent years crafting the perfect mask, the perfect disguise, the perfect identity. Strutting down the street, I would exude an air of what I thought at the time was confidence, but I realize now only looked like shame.

Underneath my carefully concealed face lay the hideous monster of self-loathing. That monster knew that the façade wasn't real. Every compliment for the mask was translated by the monster. Every bite of approval was digested into the idea that my real, authentic self was ugly. Every ounce of praise only added to the heaping pile of proof that said I needed to cover myself up. Every time someone said, "You're beautiful," I'd hear "You're ugly, keep concealing." Every time someone said, "You're so great to be around," I'd hear "You're boring, keep lying." Each compliment to the mask was a blow to my core. I, however, did not see the mask. All I saw was person after person who failed to make me feel loved.

The years before the mask were even worse. As a young girl, I would compare myself to every woman I saw. Was she prettier, skinnier, more attractive? I would watch Jennifer Aniston on the television and feel my thighs sink into the couch as I either ate or starved myself to death. It didn't matter if my stomach hurt from hunger or from gluttony. Either way, I still wasn't her. I still wasn't perfect. Through every show and every commercial break, envy would pour through me, hot and sickening. In public, it was even worse. At least on the television, I could fool myself by saying that they stretched the screen or used technology to edit the women's bodies. In real life, however, I couldn't hide behind those assumptions. The envy would bubble and burn within me, like a violent chemical reaction spilling all over my organs. Some days, it felt literally physically painful to stay in my own skin. The worst, however, the absolute worst, was facing my reflection. Often, I would avoid it at all costs. Other times, I'd stare purposefully, silently shouting insults at myself for every imperfection. My relationship with myself was the most verbally abusive relationship I've ever had.

One mid-June afternoon in my late teen years, I had my first eye-opening experience. Like most life-changing shifts in awareness, my first glimpse bred only confusion, not insight. It took years before I understood what really happened that sticky, humid afternoon. That Sunday, just like every other Sunday, my parents corralled me into their purple minivan with its nauseating leather-in-the-sunlight stench, and set off to the shopping mall. We weaved in and out of stores, my parents discussing the optimal amount of racks in a toaster oven while I wished myself invisible. We ended up in a large department store, navigating the bottom floor with its lemon-scented, tiled walkways lined by square floor-to-ceiling poles with mirrors on all sides. Department after department, I tried to keep my head down and my thoughts focused on avoiding the cracks in the tiles. I was really avoiding the silent judgment I felt radiating powerfully from the other shoppers.

There I was gliding awkwardly through the perfume department when I looked up and I saw a girl who immediately triggered that burning, raw envy. Like a shot of straight whiskey, it came down hard and washed its hot sickness into every part of my core. As she walked towards me, I eyed her skinny thighs and perfect breasts, wishing I had what she had. If only, I thought, if only I could have a body like that. Why couldn't I have been born with a body like that? She came closer. I felt my heart beating faster as I imagined her eyes drilling through my enormous, unshapely frame, silently thanking her creator that, at least, she didn't look like me. My face reddened. I felt my tense limbs surrender in helplessness. I just wanted it to stop. I just wanted to be her, and to stop being myself. I wanted to jump right out of my ugly, disgusting skin and settle into her comfortable, beautiful body.

Only when I was about to walk headfirst into the mirror did I realize that it was me. I envied myself. Confused and shocked, I walked out of the store in a strange daze. I didn't understand what happened, though I thought about it compulsively for weeks on end trying to decode the message. After a while, my confusion faded as the intensity of the experience wore off and I settled back into familiar self-deprecating patterns. For some time, I considered that, maybe, it wasn't necessary for me to hate myself so much. As the initial shock wore off, however, I just excused the memory of the incident as an illusion, an accident, a trick of the eye.

Less than half a decade later, I was unrecognizable. My hair had gone from my natural light brown to pitch black. My face was lathered in makeup and my skin infused with metal and ink. I no longer felt things like embarrassment or shame. I felt only cold distance and judgmental superiority. That self-hating girl never healed. I just pushed her down, telling her that I'd protect her by donning a protective shield. Within the mask, I was in an armoured fortress surrounded by several armies with cannons and guns. I was miles away from civilization—paranoid, cold, and hiding from the dangers that lay "out there." I didn't feel pain, but I also didn't feel joy. I didn't love anyone and I didn't love myself. I only felt a black, gaping void that became larger each year, while I tried to stuff it with anything I could find. I pumped myself full of knowledge and money, philosophy and power, chocolate and chemicals. I would get into relationships and bare myself for just a moment, but then I'd retreat. In my trigger-happy, isolated fear, I drove away anyone who tried to love me, and then blamed them.

There were times when I would look at myself in the mirror and I'd see something hiding behind those judgmental, cold eyes—something innocent and pleading. Anytime I tried to access that part of me, it got ugly, fast. Each attempt to bypass my own defence mechanisms came with barrages of painful memories, self-destructive thoughts, and so much pain I could hardly move. And so, I drowned it out. I ran into every pair of open arms and into the embrace of every vice.

My mask, like every mask eventually must, began to split. Though I filled in the cracks as well as I could, my true self was suffocating, blue-faced, and gasping for air. The more I covered up, the harder she fought to get out. I didn't understand what was happening. I felt a war going on deep inside of me. My inner self, like a caged animal, threatened to either burst out or destroy everything within. I began to contemplate suicide in-between bouts of self-destruction. Like a tornado, my self-hating thoughts and traumatic memories tore through me, sucking me deeper into where I dared not go, leading me to a place I would later call my mental breakdown, my rock bottom. A point came when I knew, suddenly and concretely, that I had to make a choice: change or die.

For hours, I sat on my bedroom floor contemplating this choice. Like Hamlet, I weighed the pros and cons of ending my life. Somehow, I found a shred of hope, a dose of strength I didn't know I had. I chose to change. As I let go, the self-loathing I had been burying within me burst out and tore through every muscle in my body. Exhausted and blinded by pain, I went to bed. Nothing could have prepared me for what came next.

The following day, I tried to carry on as usual, but I could not. I sat down to do my makeup and my hand would not move. I stared at myself, my face bare, naked. I realized for the first time that, mask or no mask, I hated myself. Why was I covering up? Who was I covering up for? If I was going to hate myself anyway, I thought, I might as well hate my real self. I took out my piercings. I left the makeup in the bag. I stripped the colour out of my hair. As I removed each layer of external protection, my disgust at myself persisted. I began to realize that this battle within me did not originate from my appearance, from my lack of beauty, from my eyebrows or my thighs. It came from my mind. It came from my thoughts about myself.

In the weeks that followed, years of repressed self-hatred pumped through my veins as I faced my bare reflection in the mirror. Everything from the pigment of my skin to the colour of my eyebrows screamed obscenities at me. I surrendered. I took the screams like inner blows, allowing them to penetrate me. For the first time in many years, I didn't drown out my feelings or cover them up. I just let them happen, and then I went on with my day. For weeks, I became gradually weaker and weaker. Taking those beatings from myself was hard and, at the time, I wasn't sure that it would all be okay. I just knew I had to do it.

The inside of my mind became a horror film. All the walls, gates, and blocks that I had put up against my thoughts were down. I had no protection from the ghosts of my past or the shadows of my psyche. The truth felt like a jagged little pill, a cruel poison. I drank it down and, no matter how much I cried or screamed, I came back for more.

One day, three or four weeks after my fateful breakdown, I came in front of the mirror with my head down. I approached like this so I could relax before I looked. I wanted to make sure that I didn't brace myself against what would come. I wanted to make sure that I didn't try to fight it. After all, I'd been fighting it for so long. Though I was weak, I took a deep breath, relaxed my shoulders, and looked up into the eyes of the most beautiful woman I'd ever seen. At that moment, I suddenly remembered that one day at the department store— the only other day I'd seen anyone like her. I've never cried like I cried that day.

And then, there was peace. There was beauty, love, and quiet, beautiful peace. For the first time in my life, there was silence. I knew that something had changed. My mind had changed. My eyes had changed. I went out that day onto a busy train and felt like I was in a magical, magnificent universe. I looked at the faces of all the strangers around me and they were just so beautiful. Every chin, collarbone, and wrist. Every shape, size, race, and gender. I was surrounded by dozens of beautiful, brilliant creatures. Among them, there was no ugliness and there was no mediocrity. Everyone was transcendent. I'd never lived in such a world with such people.

I realized, early on, that I was experiencing love, but I had no idea what love was. For a long time, I couldn't understand what had happened or how to hold onto it. I would get that feeling and then I would lose it. I would love myself and, then, I'd come crashing down. I'd have moments of peace and, then, I'd feel the war coming on again. I'd search for that feeling in my relationships with others, but the harder I looked, the less I found. This was the second part of my journey. It was my exploration into the meaning of love and the nature of it. I wanted to know what had happened to me and how I could give that experience as a gift not only to myself, but also to the world.

This was how *The Love Mindset* was born. Its conception came during a long and transformational journey throughout which I realized that my struggle with love—both for myself and for others—had nothing to do with love's availability. It had nothing to do with me either. It had nothing to do with how many pounds I weighed or whether the man across from me thought my cheeks were too big. I realized that what was really crucial about love was not me or him, you or them, today or tomorrow. The answers to love, I found, lie in the mind. The questions about love, I also found, lie within all of us, and yet we're so afraid to ask that we settle for any answer we're given.

I hope that reading this book will be as enlightening for you to read as it was for me to write. I feel honoured and privileged to be invited on your journey of healing and happiness. If you, like me, have run dry from searching for love inside romantic relationships and searching for peace in the darkness of your vices, I am glad we have found each other. Thank you for choosing me to show you the truth about who you are and what you're capable of. I am excited to share with you some insight into why you've been suffering, what love really is, and how you can, finally, live the life you want.

Always With Love,

STARVING FOR LOVE

A flower cannot blossom without sunshine, and man cannot live without love.

MAX MULLER

People all around you are dying. Perhaps you are too. Fortunately, dying isn't something we are all doing, nor is it something that we must necessarily do. We must all perish eventually, but we don't need to spend our lives perishing. People, like all other living things, spend their time on Earth either dying or growing. We cannot do both and we cannot do neither. We can make the choice to grow or die consciously or we can allow it to be made for us. Most people, however, do not only pass up this choice, they neglect to think of themselves as growing or dying. They believe themselves to be simply "living," as if living was a fixed, static state.

In this world, nothing can be static. Stability is an illusion—a mirage that arises from a trick of the eye that looks at a glimmer in time apart from its relationship to other glimmers. In the big picture, everything from the most solid-looking rock to the budding chrysanthemum is either growing or dying, building or degrading, learning or regressing.

To the rules of life, no human being is an exception. We all tend to agree that newborn babies are growing and that the sick are dying, while everyone else is put on a sort of plateau—a state of having completed growth and waiting to begin death. Such a state does not exist. This state is an illusion that allows us to slowly rob ourselves of life without any conscious awareness. In this state, people don't believe that they can grow. They think growing is for children. If they do think they can grow, they leave growth in the hands of money, success, education, and knowledge. They hear rumours that growth is a matter of mystery or luck. If you're dealt bad cards, you wither; great cards, then you prosper. These views not only distort the truth, they also do us great harm by obscuring from us the simplicity of lifelong development and fulfillment.

If I were to ask you what it means for a plant to live, you would tell me that to live is to grow. This is no different for a human being. Living is not a static state. The continuation of your livelihood immediately and automatically implies growth. If I were to then ask you what you needed to make the plant grow, you would tell me: sunlight and water. This, too, is no different for a human being. A person, like a plant, depends on his consumption of certain things to subsist. Whether we're talking about a plant or a middle-aged housewife, growth depends on an organism's intake of nourishment. To sustain life means to obtain the necessary sustenance. When we intake what we need to live, we grow. When we do not, we die. These are the rules of life.

We all know that a human being requires water, air, food, warmth, and sunlight. These are all life necessities. In order for us to grow, we must intake these in optimal amounts. If we do not, our lack begins to show. For some life necessities, such as food, it takes some time for signs of deficiency to become obvious to the onlooker. For others, such as air, it takes no time at all. If you were to come across a suffocating person, you would have no doubt about the cause of her crisis. However, if you were to come across a person who had a vitamin deficiency from neglecting his vegetables, you wouldn't be likely to deduce his plight from first glance. By the same process, you can neglect your own intake of vital nourishment, and without awareness or understanding, begin to slowly die.

Perhaps you have not realized this yet, but love is also a life necessity. When we talk about what we need to live, we list water, air, warmth, and food, but we forget about love. And who can blame us? We forget about love like we forget about the sun. It is easy to forget that the sun is what allows all our life necessities to exist. The sun causes the earth's air composition to contain the oxygen that we need to survive. The sun is what fuels the rain cycle that provides water for all the plants and, by extension, the animals that eat those plants. The sun is at the top of the chain of life necessities. It is not only vital to our survival; it is the origin of life.

Similarly, we focus on our need for approval, sex, and success. We think that, if we can become someone that others appreciate, we will get love.

This approach fails, again and again, and it fails for a reason. Can you force a wilting flower in a sunless basement to open? Of course you can. You can pry it open with your fingers; but inevitably, it will either close back up or break from the effort. What you need is not to force growth, but to feed nourishment—to expose this little piece of life to its origin. Like this, love is the essential ingredient. Without it, sex is meaningless, approval is bribery, and success is short-lived or, worse, hollow. Love is not a side effect of how we relate to ourselves and others—it is the origin of those relations. Love is not only a necessity of life; it is the origin of life. For our joy, our healing, and our relationships to be sustainable, love must come first.

*

When any living organism is deprived of something that it needs to live, it responds in one of two ways: passive submission or violent resistance. Passive submission is how trees respond to oncoming death. With each second that a tree is deprived of sunlight or water, the brilliant gloss of its leaves fades to a flat matte. With each moment, the vibrant greens shift imperceptibly along a gradient to brown. As the days go on, the twigs become more brittle, the leaves start to curl and fall off. The branches turn downwards as the plant can no longer reach its feeble arms up to receive the sun. They, too, change colour from a deep brown to a cold ash grey. With each passing sunrise, the tree slowly wilts without resistance or protest. Eventually, the last leaf falls and the last branch hardens. The plant dies, silently.

There are people all around you passively submitting to their love deficiency. As a collective, we have developed clever nouns for these death symptoms. We call them depression, low self-image, low motivation, sexual dysfunction, laziness. Without the love that sustains us, the passive sub-mitters slowly wither away. These people are often dismissed as inheritors of faulty genetics or im-proper brain chemicals. With each moment that they spend without the love that they so desper-ately need, they lose a glimmer of hope. They may realize, at one point, that love is what they need, but by that time they think it is too late or too difficult to get it. Their passion dies, along with their last shred of hope, meekly and silently.

The other response to oncoming death is violent resistance. This is the exact response that a fish displays when a fisherman grabs her out of the water. At first, the fish feels the hook in her mouth and begins to protest. As the line reels in, she panics. Her movements become jerky and volatile. She thrashes side to side, up and down. She struggles with all her might, trying one strategy, then the next, then the next. The less oxygen she receives, the harder she pushes. Feeling her impending doom drawing nearer by the millisecond, the fish fights without holding back or stopping, until her little heart burns out from a lack of oxygen. She dies quickly and suddenly, mid-battle.

All around you, there are people violently resisting their deprivation of love. We have developed clever nouns for their symptoms as well. Violent resisters display anxiety, anger, aggression, addiction, binge eating, desperation, self-harm. Sometimes, this death response is glamorized. After all, he who dies mid-battle is said to die an honourable death. There are crazed cults formed around belligerent rock stars and junkie poets. Their self-destruction is romanticized as a logical partner of their brilliance. Perhaps violent resistance is more exciting because, unlike passive submission, it seems to exude control. In truth, there is no control in either submitting or resisting. Both are symptoms of the same disease. Violent resistance just puts on a more exciting show.

As a collective, we have so deeply normalized these symptoms that our first line of defence against them is simply to remove them from sight. Day after day, more and more medications are prescribed for depression and anxiety, assuming that these things run in our blood, when really they run in our patterns of awareness. Our bodies signal to us that we are starving for love, but since we do not speak the language of the body, we become frustrated with its communication attempts. We silence ourselves with medications and vices while our grudges grow like malignant tumours, reported violence spreads like a virus, and mood disorders continue to rise to the highest levels in recorded history. We continue to treat the symptoms, but we do not treat the problem, so the problem grows. It's like we are attempting to clean oil out of the ocean, while the spill keeps flowing, and no one bothers to find the source. We just clean up the mess the best we can and accept it as a part of life.

We conceal our symptoms of love deprivation with medications, and why wouldn't we? If you were asked to choose between a lifetime of pain and a lifetime of taking pills for that pain, what would you choose? Even those who, like my past self, refuse the doctor's orders will often self-medicate with illegal drugs, alcohol, food, sex—anything to take the edge off. The problem, then, is not with the medications, the doctors, or the medical system. The problem is not even that we're overmedicating ourselves. The real problem is that we have collectively accepted love deprivation as a normal state—just the way life is. We do not acknowledge it, so we cannot address it. We silence the symptoms, while we forget the cause.

Of course, love alone will not magically cure every kind of mental and emotional health issue. Giving a plant sunlight and water may not be enough. It might need worms, bees, or a different climate. However, without the sun, the plant cannot and will not thrive. By giving a thousand dying plants sunlight and water as a first response, we can then attend individually to those that need something else as well. Of course, love is not the one magic pill that will fix everything forever. Nothing is like that, despite how ardently modern-day marketers try to convince us of this. But if we can find a way to tend to love deprivation as a first response, rather than an irrelevant detail or an afterthought, we will heal so much of the pain in the world that, whatever is left, we will actually have the time and resources to address. By acknowledging and attending to love deprivation as a real cause of suffering, we will find ourselves closer than ever before to building a society that is conducive to lifelong happiness.

2

WHAT LOVE IS

Love is misunderstood to be an emotion; actually, it is a state of awareness, how we see ourselves and how we see our relationships with others.

DAVID R. HAWKINS

I used to think that love was a feeling brought on by other people. When I got that feeling, I was ecstatic. I felt worthy, beautiful, and alive. I would be kind and generous to my lover, but secretly I would dread the day that he would get tired of me and stop giving me that feeling. I would say, "I love you," but I really meant, "Don't leave me." With each failed relationship, my definition of love would warp slightly. First, love was just a rumour.

Then, love was the blood in my veins and the air in my lungs. Then, love was a drug. Then, love was an addiction. Then, love was pain. Then, love was a lie.

Suddenly, after my mask came off, love was all that mattered. When I suddenly saw myself and other people as beautiful and powerful, I realized, early on, that this was love. With each day after my initial awakening, the feeling faded a little bit more. I grasped for it, desperately, wanting nothing more than to feel that deep, healing love for the rest of my life. And yet, there was a problem. Even though I wanted love more than anything in the world, I still didn't understand what it was, where it came from, or how to get it back. My greatest goal in life was to attain something that I couldn't define or understand. If that's not setting yourself up for failure, I don't know what is.

I developed theories, but they all fell through. If the feeling of love was something that came from being loved, why did I get it in an empty room? If this feeling came from my relationship with myself, then why did it persist when I went out? And, more importantly, why did it fade over time, even though I kept looking at myself in the mirror just the same way? If love was a choice, then why couldn't I choose to feel that same powerful connection again? I was lost. No matter what I did, I just couldn't seem to reproduce the feeling I so desperately wanted. Out of my confused frustration grew the seeds of obsession.

I wanted answers and I wanted them badly; however, I was unwilling to look into the corners where they lay. I searched psychology up and down. I looked in relationship books. I trusted science and I looked deeply into study after study for answers. Yet none came. Then, I looked to philosophy and I still had nothing to sink my teeth into. Once in a while, I'd come across spiritual ideas, but I'd ignore them. For me, spirituality was out of the question. I grew up being admired for my IQ, my ability to get high grades, my logical reasoning. I thought all of that look-into-your-heart-open-your-soul stuff was the brain food of the uneducated. I thought the answers to my questions would come in the form of numbers and concrete facts, because that was the only way I knew to receive answers. I drove myself crazy looking for answers to a spiritual question in the material world.

At this point, I started carrying a voice recorder with me. Everywhere I went, from the city street on a Friday night to the isolated cabin up north, I brought my question: "What is love?" I asked again and again, hoping to, one day, run into a definition that made any sense to me. This went on for several months. The definitions I received coloured the gradient from roll-your-eyes immature to deeply profound. People's definitions of love are as infinite as their personal experiences of it.

The definition that came to have the largest impact on me came from a stranger on the beach. After months of furious obsession, during which I consumed hundreds of ideas from just as many sources, clarity came in the strangest of packages.

That fateful afternoon, I was nestled in the sand (writing a chapter of a very different sort of book) when he came up to talk to me. At first glance, he didn't look like the bringer of epiphany. He was covered in dirt, smoking a cigarette, and reeked badly of alcohol. He was extremely angry and gesturing wildly with his open flask of whiskey. Over the course of the next half hour, he revealed to me that he'd been released that very same day from the mental health wing of a maximum-security prison in Northern Ontario. His grammar was poor and his words slurred. He alternated between yelling and crying. He told me that he'd just come home to find that, in his absence, his wife had left him for another man. She wouldn't let him in and told him he'd never be able to see his daughter again. He told me he'd spent the last 20 years in and out of prisons and hospitals. He spent each day counting down to the moment that he would be able to see his family again. Now, he was finally free. Now, he could go home, but he didn't have a home to go to. He apologized for crying.

After a while, his movements became less aggressive and he seemed to have released his pent up frustration. Calmer and more settled, we sat in silence as he stared towards the horizon. After a few minutes, he said that he should probably go. He thanked me for listening and turned to walk away. Suddenly, he turned back around and asked me if there was anything he could do to thank me. He suggested a shot of whiskey, haphazardly holding out his flask. I politely declined and instead pulled out my voice recorder. I asked him to tell me what he thought love was. He thought for a moment and then he said, "Love is the most important thing."

He swayed a bit and went silent. Having heard this before, I wasn't enthused. I hadn't really been expecting much in any case. I sighed, smiled, and was about to push the little red "Stop" button when he said, "Wait, I'll even explain."

He paused again, and then continued speaking slowly, enunciating clearer than he had throughout the past hour.

"Love's when you meet somebody and you look at them, and there's a moment right there. You just pick up on it and you just know. There's something there. You see it. You know it. You actually feel it going through your body. You know it's there. You hold it. You grasp it. You keep it safe."

After that, he left. I'll never forget the way I felt as I sat there in the July sunshine. Suddenly, I felt clear. Rapidly, everything started making sense. I sat there half-paralyzed for hours while I played the incident over and over in my head and the recording over and over in my ear. Love, I realized for the first time, was a form of unity. It was a connection—the only connection that we all truly have in common. In the absence of all similarities, love remains dominant. Everything that isn't love is just like tassels—decorative, optional. Love is the foundation for equality, peace, and harmony. It really is the most important thing.

Staring at his path after he left, I realized that I loved that man. I watched people walk by on the boardwalk in the warm summer sun and I realized that I loved them too. Listening to his words again and again on my recorder, "... when you meet somebody ... and you just know." I got up and walked, dozens of strangers becoming that somebody. Everyone I looked at, there was a moment and I just knew that there was something there. There was that feeling that I'd spent my whole life, especially the past few months, desperately searching for, thinking I had to fight or beg for it, igniting with stranger after stranger. It wasn't lust or desire or envy. It was love. Real, true love.

*

How many of us have painful experiences with love, and then we define love as painful? How many of us experience abuse, abandonment, or disappointment from love, and then place those characteristics on love itself? For most of my life, I had thought of love as a feeling, as something that happened to me, as an experience—but I never thought to ask where that experience came from. I judged love, because I misunderstood what it was.

We may experience love, but love is not an experience. Love is what we see when we turn our attention towards the interconnected pattern that connects us with all living things. In any given moment, there is a densely interrelated harmony, an interdependent unity, between all the elements of every thriving ecosystem, and between all ecosystems. In every environment, there is a background of unified, self-perpetuating cycles that keep each element in that environment full of life. Love is the origin of life and the purpose of life. It is where all things come from and what they return to.

We tend to mistake love for something temporary and elusive. We even represent our so-called love with things like roses—vibrant one moment and dead the next. This is not the true nature of love. Love is like the sun. It does not depend on us to sustain it, nor is it something we've created. It is ever-present and abundant. It is we who are confused. Yet our confusion does not change love.

The sun was not dimmer before we understood its function. Most living things, in fact, do not have the capacity to understand the sun's (or any other thing's) "function." This does not affect the sun one bit. Love is the same way. No matter how much we ignore it or pretend it does not exist, it does not fade. No matter how many times we say "love" when we mean sexual attraction, addiction, or some other thing, love does not change.

People tend to think that relationships are static and that love is what varies. It is the opposite. Love is what is eternal and ever-present. Nothing that abides by the rules of life can be static. Love, however, does not play by the same rules. It is not something that grows and dies like all other living things. It is the origin of life and its purpose. Among all that is impermanent, love stays the same.

Why, then, does it feel like love comes and goes from day to day, person to person? Love comes and goes like the sun rises and sets. The sun doesn't really disappear when it goes down. It simply goes out of view. Every day, the sun rises and every night the sun sets. The sun, however, stays in the same form. It is not the actual sun that rises and sets. It is not the sun that turns red or orange. It is our perception of it from where we're standing that changes. Love is like this too. Love flows abundantly and eternally. What changes is our perception of it. Our awareness changes depending on where we're coming from and, thus, love takes on all sorts of adjectives, meanings, and forms.

A sunset may look similar to a group of people in the same city, while love may look completely different to two people in the same room. When we are trying to look at something that involves us so deeply and directly, our own position has much more power over our awareness. We cannot see the whole universe while being a tiny speck within it.

I tried so hard for so long to make myself experience love, like love was something that did not exist until I gave it existence, like I was in control of it. But love, to flow, has never needed my acknowledgement or approval.

The sun doesn't care if you dislike its rays on your face. It will keep shining. The sun also does not care if a neighbour's tree is casting a shade over your garden. Of course, that situation may be frustrating. It may cause you to get upset and scream. You can yell all you want, but the sun will shine as it shines. If your garden is not in the sun's rays, no amount of blaming the sun will solve the problem. Its rays will not go around objects or through them. You can never expect the sun to change itself for you. It will shine as it shines, completely oblivious to whether or not you're attending to it or using its rays to the best of your ability. It shone the same when we clubbed one another over the head, and it will continue to shine the same now. And so it goes with love.

In our ignorance about the nature of love, most of us have bought into a most dangerous myth: that love is scarce. I once believed this with all my heart. I thought that some people, in their lives, would get love, and some wouldn't. If you were lucky enough to have loving parents or to meet the right person, you'd get love. If not, you wouldn't. That was just the way things were. Or so I thought. This simple misunderstanding led me to the world of codependence, violence, and abuse.

When the love hungry get a glimpse of what they need, they fear it's the only scrap they'll ever get, so they hold on with all their might. They hold on to those who hurt them. They hold on to those who don't want them. They hold on to those who don't hurt them and who do want them, but they hold on so tight that they suffocate their lovers and drive them away.

Centuries ago, there lived people who believed that there was a scarcity of food just as much as we've believed that there's a scarcity of love. They grasped for scraps of bones with the same desperation that we grasp for a few words of approval. They threw themselves at prey the way we throw ourselves at each other, all of us desperate to satisfy our hunger.

To the nomadic tribe that has scoured an area and decided to move on, it seems obvious that there is a lack of resources. Their next spot will be bountiful as well, until it runs dry. But what if, instead of hunting and gathering on their new land, the nomads undertake agriculture? What if the tribe settles, learns to farm, and begins to produce sustainable resources? Then, there would be no shortage of food after all. And, in fact, there was never any shortage of the potential supply of food. There was only a shortage of knowledge about how to harness that supply.

Imagine not knowing this. Imagine wandering from place to place, starving, never knowing how to cultivate sustainable nourishment. Is this the relationship you have had with love? Is this what you have believed, like I believed, was the problem? Were you taught to cling to scraps of limited love

instead of being taught to harness the infinite supply of love that has always been available to you?

Nowadays, there are still many cultures that
are deprived of food. Curiously enough, many of
these cultures have no deprivation of love. They
balance their lack of one life necessity with an
abundance of another. Those who starve for love do
the same. No one is satisfied. Like this, our culture
has bred consumers and addicts. We eat too much,
buy too much, and want too much. We set ourselves on the fruitless mission of filling the gaping
hole within us with material things. Blindly, we
consume more and more, believing we are hungry
for more food, status, or money, yet really we are
hungry for connection. The hole widens, bottomless
to all of our invented pleasures, and craving only
the nourishment of love.

If only we all knew that love, like food, is
simple if we learn the rules of how it works. If only
it was common knowledge that love is a basic necessity. If only we recognized the myth of love
scarcity as false and the symptoms of love deprivation as responsible for many of our problems. If
only we practiced understanding our own suffering
and the suffering of others with non-judgment and

compassion. If only we were all taught from childhood that love is just like the sun—it is all around us, keeping us alive, and we need only to adjust ourselves to its nature to get the harvest we wish to—and need to—reap.

We have misunderstood love. Love is not temporary, rare, and limited. Love is more abundant than we could possibly imagine. Just like there is more air than we could possibly breathe in, there is more love than we could possibly perceive. There is no risk of running out of love. There is no limit on love. The only limits are of our perception, our awareness. The only risk is being closed off to love and living a life of failing to perceive it.

*

As a human being, you have the ability to not only participate in the interconnected nature of our universe, but also to be aware of that nature and aware of your participation. Take a moment to realize what an incredible gift this is. You have evolved past mere survival, past pure instinct. You have the ability to ponder, to wonder, to appreciate. Our distant ancestors could not do this. Most living things cannot do this. They are part of the unity, but they cannot marvel at it or deliberately impact it. A lizard, for example, reacts automatically, mechanically, in response to her environment without any ability to meditate a while on her role in all of existence and then make conscious decisions about her behaviours based on what she perceives. The lizard is completely engrossed in the present moment without any awareness of it. Thus, unity is there, but it eludes her.

There are many animals that show loving behaviours towards one another as well as towards us, such as dogs, cats, primates. And yet, how many of these animals can become aware of their connection to everything that ever was, is, and will be? How many of them can purposefully cultivate a sense of compassion towards those who hurt them, and not just their relatives or children, but towards all living beings? How many other creatures can become aware of their harmony with each leaf, each rock, each stream, each moment—and then communicate about this awareness to one another? How many other species have the ability to not only empathize with other organisms, but the power to take action to help them?

THE LOVE MINDSET

By being born human, we have been given a gift, but most of us have not unwrapped this gift. We have this incredible ability to shift our awareness, purposefully, towards the interrelated pattern that binds us to everything and everyone. We have the power to experience universal, unwavering love. How many of us are making full use of this ability? How many of us are using our powers of awareness to obsess over the past, worry about the future, and distort the world to match our false understanding of it? We have acquired the ability to be aware of our connection to the universe, and with that, we have acquired the ability to be completely unaware of it. On this journey of evolution, some of us have stopped halfway.

Most people love in a way that is far inferior to what we are capable of. Their "love" is conditional and selective. They love some people and not others. Those whom they claim to love, they'll claim to be indifferent to the next moment because they didn't get what they wanted from that person. Worst of all, they wait to be given love by someone, starving in the interim. We are capable of so much more, and yet we do not realize how much we can do, nor how badly we need to do it.

Evolution happens with or without us. Evolution is happening now. Our collective awareness of our nature is in its budding stages. Just like our opposable thumbs were weak when we first received them, our love awareness is weak. In order for us to capitalize on our newfound gift from evolution, we must understand it, train it, and sacrifice the comfort of old patterns for the vast possibilities of new ones. Our ability to ignore love makes us suffer, but our suffering is not for nothing. It is a call from our deepest potential and the call says: evolve.

Think of the journey we've made, in the first world, from the caveman to the grocery store shopper. The process of feeding ourselves once consumed most of our time, closely followed by escaping predators and finding shelter. Thousands of years later, the need for food only crosses our minds a few times a day and is easily fulfilled. Now, we're finding love like we, at one point, found agriculture. It's new, fresh, and exciting. It's unfamiliar, frightening, and full of promise.

The practice of agriculture has rewarded us with time. We would not have such elaborate systems of art, education, or entertainment if we were all too busy hunting and foraging. That one simple discovery—the discovery of how to harness the power of a constant, ever-present source of livelihood to our advantage—has made a monumental difference in our lives. Learning to harness the power of love will do the same. It will completely change the way that we relate to one another and to our own selves. Our suffering, our starvation, our desperation—these are not symptoms of hopelessness. These are symptoms of stagnation. We have been stuck in love scarcity for too long. We must move on, adapt, and evolve into our potential. The next stage of evolution is the evolution of perception, the evolution of the mind. The future of our personal, spiritual, and communal development lies our expanding awareness of our connection to one another, to the Earth, and to all that exists.

3

LOVING WITH THE MIND

It is slavery to live in the mind unless it has become part of the body.

KHALIL GIBRAN

When we speak of love, we often speak of the heart. We say we are heartbroken or that our hearts have been wounded. We say that our heart was stolen or captured. We claim to have given our heart away. We say that she wears her heart on her sleeve. We tell him to put his heart into it. We give the heart characteristics like light or dark, soft or hardened, big or small.

We do not make these comparisons simply to sound poetic. Our heart-centred expressions are actually metaphors for our feelings. When we feel intense emotions, we often feel them in our chests. For this reason, people speak of opening their hearts to love. In a relationship, we symbolically offer each other our hearts. This sort of gift represents devotion and commitment. To give your heart to someone appears to be the highest privilege that you can bestow upon a person.

While talk of the heart whispers of romance, it is largely inaccurate. Obviously, you cannot literally give someone your heart, nor can you open it. That would mean death. However, you can't do it symbolically or metaphorically either. If the heart represents your emotions, you can't give someone your emotions. Nor can you promise anyone that you will continue to feel the same emotions in five years. This would be as ludicrous as saying that you'll always enjoy your friend's cooking, regardless of what dish she makes or which ingredients she uses. You could predict your enjoyment, but you could never promise it with certainty. You may think you can, but your taste buds will not follow your orders so easily. Your emotions, like your tastes, are not under your conscious control.

But that doesn't stop us from trying to control our emotions, does it? Again and again, we fail at controlling our feelings, and again and again, we try. We try to make ourselves feel happy, but the miserable thoughts sink their teeth into every glimmer of hope. We try to make ourselves feel peaceful, to let go, to no avail. We try to become attracted to people who are good for us. We try to feel cool and confident. We try to make ourselves feel passion for work we can't help but hate.

We fail at feeling the emotions we want, and we fail at suppressing the ones we don't want. We fall in love with the wrong people—people who hurt us. We feel shame, rejection, embarrassment, and no matter how much we resist, our faces give us away. We feel anger bubbling, and no matter how many times we push it down, it only comes back stronger and more powerful. We overflow with self-loathing, disgust, helplessness. We try to resist our cravings, our compulsions, our self-destructive urges. We can only resist for so long. Desperately, we try and try to control our emotions, but we fail, and we fail for a reason. You and I, and all of us—we don't control our hearts.

You, as a human being, are like a tree. Your emotions are like the fruits on this tree. You cannot summon them into being, nor keep them from flourishing simply by doing something to the fruits themselves. The difference between rotten apples and sweet apples cannot be made by altering the apples. In order to change the quality of the fruit, you must change the way that you care for the rest of the tree. The fruit will change accordingly, as a by-product.

To be open to love, you must open your heart, but this cannot be done through the heart itself. The heart is a muscle. Like other muscles, it changes only when you do other things. The muscles on your body get bigger when you exercise and smaller when you do not. When they get bigger, you naturally feel stronger and healthier. This is your body's way of telling you that you're doing something good and you should continue. The heart is the same with love. Your heart gives you pleasant emotions when you're open to love and unpleasant ones when you are not. When you are open, you feel safe, connected, and powerful. The wisdom of nature ensures that, when we fulfill our desires and our potential, we get a reward for it.

Remember, however, that the rewards—the muscles and the emotions—are only by-products. The heart is simply a signal mechanism that is not under our conscious control. In order to sway the heart, to open it to love, we must look elsewhere.

If we want to feed a tree the nutrients it requires, we must feed those parts of it that accept nutrients. If we pour water onto the trunk or we cover up the leaves from sunlight, only allowing the rays to hit the ground, this will not make a plant healthy. We must feed life energy into the places where it can be absorbed. On a tree, water first comes in through the roots and sunlight first comes in through the leaves. In a human being, love first comes in through the mind.

*

I came into my understanding of love and the mind through experience. Only after my experiences, I found the field of spirituality, waiting with many points of agreement, and just as many points of contention. In some spiritual traditions, especially those of the East, the mind has earned a rotten reputation. While they honour the heart with traits such as courageous, loving, and gentle, they label the mind as egotistical, judgmental, and authoritative. They decorate the heart with the wisdom of faith and true understanding, while they dismiss the mind as a coercive two-year-old who must get his way or an eager five-year-old who asks too many questions. The message they send to the mind is: thanks for all your overthinking and overanalyzing, but we'll be transcending you now. You're much too critical and logical. We need something more spiritual, loving, and kind. We need not think, but feel, act, and experience. You, mind, cannot possibly understand love, joy, or enlightenment because all you do is worry, fear, and project. When it comes to love, you're to be silenced, tamed, and suppressed. With the pesky mind out of the way, we can travel the path of love, in word and deed. Love, these gurus say, is a place the mind cannot go.

In other spiritual traditions, the mind is given more power and more importance. They say: don't think those bad thoughts, think good ones. Believe in all the correct things, not the wrong things. Purity of heart is dependent on a person's ability to think pure thoughts. A person is good or bad depending on if his beliefs are good or bad.

Last year, close to Christmas, in the midst of polite small talk typical for this time of year, my conversation partner asked me if I was going to church. I said I was considering it.

"Are you Christian?" he asked.

"I wouldn't call myself that," I replied, "but I do subscribe to the teachings of Christ, among others. I'd say I abide by the fundamental morals of every religion and the inner core of every spiritual tradition."

He paused, his eyes darting around for some way to comprehend my words. After a few moments, with his brow furrowed, he slowly asked, "So, not a Christian, then?"

After I discovered that my mental breakdown and subsequent experience of universal love was often called a "spiritual awakening," I explored many avenues of spirituality. I found myself believing all of them, and none of them, at once. I could not believe that the mind could be transcended. How can we continue to perceive beyond the sensory experiences allowed to us by our brains? Even if we are spiritual beings, how can we experience ourselves in any other way except through the anatomy of these human bodies we're living in? I also could not believe that the only thing we needed to do was to feed our minds the "right" thoughts. Who says they are right? Under what authority are we to call some thoughts good and others bad? I hadn't achieved my feeling of interconnectedness through reciting dogma or reading someone else's ideas of what was right and wrong. What happened to me was something natural, something organic, something that happened before I knew what was happening. I never tried to silence or transcend my mind. I was not trying to "be good" or "think good thoughts." I simply allowed myself to experience the pain that naturally came from thinking one way, and to experience the pleasure that naturally came from perceiving another way. I allowed my mind and heart to do their work. I did not try to force myself into any pre-existing ideas of what a "spiritual" person should do or think. I simply surrendered to a higher process.

I am pro-mind. The mind, I believe, is a vital part of our evolution, even though it has led many of us astray from our inner wisdom. The mind is not good or bad. It is a tool which must be used in such a way that it returns us to our most courageous, loving, and eternal selves. A loving mind

36

gives us a loving heart from which we can easily do loving deeds and say loving words. The mind is meant to drive us towards our ultimate potential, not impede it. Alas, it is capable of both.

The optimal functioning of the mind is as a control centre, as a leader. The most effective leaders listen to the people and adapt to their needs. The successful leader sets goals and plans based on the community's struggles and hopes. This is the mind at its finest. It is, as dualists say, necessary to use the mind and to use it in a specific way. It is also, as the non-dualists say, necessary to connect to oneself, others, and reality by way of experience.

Most of us misunderstand the mind. Those who seek spiritual progress, whether or not their beliefs serve them, at least put some thought into the relationship between their inner world and their outside experience. Most people, however, give the mind no thought. They misunderstand it by default. They function automatically, doing whatever they have been conditioned to do. Their whole existence revolves around seeking pleasure and avoiding pain, without any awareness of this process. There is no understanding, only automatic responding.

THE LOVE MINDSET

Misunderstanding often accompanies misuse. For most people, the mind is like a complicated piece of technology for which they don't have a user's guide. They may be able to execute a few small tasks, but they keep running into walls trying to make the device do what they want it to do. Not only can they not use it in a basic sense, they cannot possibly reap the benefits of the advanced functions. Such a person is especially vulnerable to the influence of authorities bearing answers.

Like this, people who misunderstand their minds either relinquish control to whomever desires the reins or they fight ceaselessly against themselves. Much like our response to love deprivation, our response to the mind is either passive submission or violent resistance. We surrender in ignorance or we struggle in confusion.

The misunderstood mind is like a corrupt system of government. Most people feel powerless in its wake. Many people do nothing. They don't vote. They don't act. They don't care. Some do only what other people are doing. During election season, they bicker over candidates and put in the time to vote. When the election is over, the helplessness resumes. They submit, seeing no other choice. Inevitably, there are also plenty of violent resisters who become indignant, angry, and forceful. They do manage to draw more attention to the problem, but the wheels keep going round and round. In the end, neither violence nor obedience helps. This is how most people approach their minds.

Just like government, the mind is not inherently wrong simply because it's been used improperly. Just as we cannot descend our entire system into anarchy overnight to solve the problem of power inequality, we cannot turn off our minds to solve the problems of suffering and judgment. The solutions lie in understanding and proper usage, not in helplessly ignoring or furiously resisting the alleged problem. Neither method gets us anywhere except further away from ourselves and further away from each other.

People who don't know how to use their minds cannot really know how to use their hearts either. Other animals will automatically function in synchronicity with the environment. The unity between them and the rest of the world is a natural part of their instincts and they have no choice but to follow them. Human beings, however, are not in the same boat. Humans who are not using their minds effectively are not necessarily living in harmony with the environment. Our ability to use our minds to think, focus, and attend to certain things means that we can live without attending to the unity all around us. We are like puzzle pieces who are perfectly suited to make a giant picture together, but we are assembling ourselves in the dark. Sometimes we fit and sometimes we don't. When we do, it's often an accident.

Those who try to erase the power of the mind actually fare much better than those who neglect the mind completely. Those who say they are transcending the mind are usually more open to unity. They tend to feel connected with others and to see their small part in the giant order of things. The misconception here, however, is that they have achieved this by ridding themselves of the mind. The mind is a doorway; they have simply opened the door, but this does not mean the doorway isn't there. No person can seek out teachers of enlightenment, nor follow those teachers' advice, without the mind. They cannot wilfully practice transcending it (nor convince themselves that they've done so) without the cunning of the mind. No human can function outside his mind just like no human can sprout wings and fly. We are built as we are built. However, just like we can build planes to fly, we can use the mind to experience what is beyond it. There is no transcending our minds, only using them optimally — to return to truth, to love.

The greatest potential we have for opening our hearts lies in the opening of our minds. The heart is simply a bank of emotional potential. It's a vastness of possible experience. We all hold within us the capacity for joy, love, and laughter, but not everyone uses that capacity. In order to use it, we need to reach a unity between heart and mind. In our thoughts, we hold the key to our feelings. In our minds, we hold the key to love. In the wise words of the Buddha: "All that we are is the result of what we have thought. The mind is everything. What we think we become."

In this lies the next wave of our evolution. It is not biological; it is mental. We will unite the knowledge of East and West. The West has incredible technological intelligence. This helps us create, analyze, and understand. This book would not be in your hands without this precious intelligence. By itself, however, it can steer us away from our most important core. We need to add the wisdom of the

East. This is another kind of intelligence. I call it flower intelligence—the ability to exist without struggling. The unity between both is the next wave of evolution. The unity of both *is* the love mindset.

*

Mind-opening is a process of developing awareness. Awareness is a perceptual state. To be aware of is, plainly, to notice. Love awareness is a state of mind that involves perceiving our ever-present interconnectedness to everything and everyone as we drift through life, moment to moment. She who has love awareness perceives love through all her senses. Like green leaves soak up the sun, the love-minded soak up love. The loving feelings that we receive when we direct our attention to the love all around us help to solidify this process. The more we receive, the easier it becomes.

Learning to love with the mind is like learning to walk. At first, it is painstaking and difficult. Love stands waiting for us, patient and unmoving, as we continue to return again and again. After some time, loving becomes more natural. Instead of automatically closing down around some people and situations, we begin to automatically stay open.

This practice expands, more and more, into our daily lives. The more we live, the more we love.

With sustained practice and patience, we train our minds to reach for love each time that we lose our perspective of it. Instead of our love hunger automatically triggering self-destructive reflexes, with practice, our natural response to love deprivation becomes love awareness. The love mindset is like a compass that always points to love. I always know how to get back home to myself, back home to reality, no matter how lost I get.

As love awareness becomes easier and we don't need to put all of our energy into consciously redirecting our minds anymore, then we can use our consciousness for something else. We can pursue our dreams and speak our truth. We can take risks and overcome our fears. We can dance, with awe-filled wonderment, in the swirling magic of the present moment.

Mind-opening is the process of developing resilience. The mind is much like the roots of a tree. When a tree is young, it is brittle. A gust of wind will easily uproot the young plant. As the tree grows older, it becomes more durable. Above the ground, its vigour shows in strong branches and healthy leaves. This is not, however, the secret behind the tree's resilience. The secret to its withstanding fierce winds lies in the thickness of the roots—unseen and powerful—which keep it grounded. The secrets of sustainability are not in plain sight for either a tree or a person. The secret of mindset, of sustained awareness, lies within each person who has ever healed and found happiness.

4

ADDICTED TO TRIGGERS

*Love is but the discovery of ourselves in others, and the
delight in the recognition.*

ALEXANDER SMITH

A mind open to love, for most, has been the rainbow of pleasures — rare, elusive, and beautiful. It is a state that many of us have entered without conscious will, driven simply by our deep hunger for connection. Like a hungry tiger enters into a deprivation-induced state where his only drive is to eat, we enter such states with love. Desperate for connection, we forget all else and set out to hunt for it. What we seek, we find. Sometimes, we find the connection we so deeply desire with a lover. Other times we find it at the bottom of a bottle. Then, when morning comes and the rush is over, we're hungry once again. Yesterday's meal is gone and it is time to hunt for another.

Most people, having no way to steadily access the love that they so deeply desire, settle for a small bite here and there. They're never satisfied. They get just enough to keep them alive, to keep them hunting. Sadly, most people spend very little of their lives in love awareness, and the little time they do spend is accidental. Each time the accident occurs, they feel they've found the answer to all their problems. Then, the waves of nourishing pleasure are gone as fast as they came, leaving nothing but frustration and confusion. Love awareness, for most, is not an intentionally cultivated state of mind, but a triggered one.

Our ignorance about the nature of love reveals itself in our language. We do not call our love awareness by its name nor by the same name each time it is triggered. We name each instance specifically by the trigger, not by the state itself. We call it trust, friendship, commitment, excitement. We call it rapport and relationship. We call it compatibility, affinity, fate. Each time we call it something, we relate it to what we believe caused the state and we place the responsibility for our happiness into the hands of the trigger. I do not simply love; I must love something or someone. I am not just happy; I must be happy about something. We are not just united; we are united in the name of some cause. We aren't just connected, you and I; we've got to have something in common. It isn't just you, as you are, that makes you my friend, lover, or comrade; it is something that you've done. You've earned my trust, my love, my friendship. All is conditional and all is temporary.

Our understanding of the fundamentals of human happiness is reminiscent of mythology. Having no idea about our true nature, or the nature of love, we invent stories about why, sometimes, we're happy and why, other times, we're sad. We tell tales about why some relationships work and others do not. We pass down myths, friend to friend, generation to generation, about human nature, relationships, and potential. Such a pattern is common with matters that are poorly understood. The less people know, the more they talk. The less people understand, the more they try to explain.

THE LOVE MINDSET

Our most common tale says that love comes from romantic relationships. This story is then accessorized with advice about how to find the perfect partner and how to act with that partner in order to keep the love circulating. Love, in our current mythology, is the by-product of having made the correct choices. When we lose the feeling of love, we switch partners or we try some tricks from our favourite magazine to keep the love alive. For a moment, it really works. Then, the trigger—like every trigger—fades, and we're back to where we started. Instead of questioning our rhetoric about love, we plunge our hands back into the pile of relationship advice once again.

For some, this process is too painful. Triggering in and out of love awareness with romantic partners is too shame-inducing for some, so they begin to seek it elsewhere. They find triggers in friends and foods, drugs and songs. In our love-hungry culture, how many people have settled for being triggered by television characters and celebrities? How many have found love by becoming fanatic fans or devoted worshippers? And how many of us, when we discover a new trigger, feel the need to tell everyone we know about it?

Behind all our ignorance, there is a beautiful, authentic tendency for us to share our ideas about love. We feel, for a moment, the blissful nourishment of love awareness and we want to spread our joy to others. Many songs and books, paintings and buildings, therapies and religions have been founded on this intention. As a result, most of us have dozens, if not hundreds, of poorly segmented ideas about how to get that coveted feeling. Behind many of our self-destructive, self-defeating rituals lies the intention to experience a connection to the world. The desire to be loved, to feel loved, is behind every diet, pill, surgery, and lie. It is behind each act of violence and every affair as well as each organized religion and every method of self-help.

We say that we are seeking happiness, joy, fun, love, comfort, safety, excitement, passion, arousal, trust. These are all versions of the same concept: health. Hungry for the love that sustains us, we hunt for the feelings of well-being that we get when we receive it. It does not occur to us to link these triggers to the same need. People go to a job to get money, when really it's about love. People go on diets to get skinny, when really it's about love. People go to a baseball game thinking they love the game, yet really it's about love. People do drugs and drink themselves to death—and that's about love too.

Since love is a life necessity, our experiences of receiving it are deeply satisfying. We are predators, remembering where our last meal came from and coming back there to hunt the next day. The problem is that, if not today, then next week, the prey catches on and moves over. Our hunt for love is never finished. We always find ourselves back in the same spot, empty-handed and confused. We keep thinking we've found the answer, yet really we've just found a trigger. Then, we become hopelessly addicted to our triggers, never knowing that we can trigger ourselves.

Whether we have been triggered into happiness by meaningful contribution or passionate sensuality, the history of our happiness is the history of our feeling connected. The thread that is woven through all our joy is the thread of love. The needle that pieces our experience is similarity. We are triggered by outside proof of a connection which we don't realize already exists.

When we find ourselves dancing to the same tune, speaking the same language, or reading on the same page, we are overwhelmed with pleasure. When we hunt for love, what we hunt for is similarity. This can come in many forms. We can be triggered by similar interests, shared memories, bonding experiences, or just by being in the same place at the same time. We can be triggered by common understanding or equal levels of intoxication. Each commonality that we acknowledge between ourselves and another person acts as a sedative for the mind's protective mechanisms. You find sameness and your mind loosens slightly, opening ever so gently to allow the breeze of love to blow through you. Fuelled by pleasurable emotions, you search for further similarities. When you inevitably find what you seek, the mind relaxes more and more. Before you know it, you feel in deep sync with the person in front of you. You come to be completely open to everything he says and does, even if he says and does things you would not tolerate in a stranger. After you find enough similarities with someone, you can accept her unconditionally. This is love awareness.

This process is the basis for most therapies and religions. When people are suffering, they are isolated. They feel separated, alone, and disconnected. In any ten step instruction manual and every book of doctrines, there is complex advice that serves the very simple function of helping the lonely person find some similarity with the world around him. He connects and, suddenly, there is a burst of joy, a ray of hope. He believes that it was those steps or that book, specifically, that brought him happiness, when really he has simply been triggered into his natural state. The reason many people spend their lifetimes dedicated to an organized religion is because they find themselves in a community of people who are constantly triggering one another, constantly finding unity under the basis of some belief. There are few things more powerful than people united. What they unite over is not what matters. The trigger is irrelevant, interchangeable, and unnecessary. The most important aspect is remembering our existing connection, and, through that, allowing ourselves to feel at peace.

If we understand our ever-present connection with all human beings, we will feel love in the presence of all people. If, on the other hand, we limit ourselves by only acknowledging our connection to others when we perceive similarities, our minds, and therefore our hearts, will only open when we find what we think we're looking for. Think of the bad first impression—you meet someone, your mind searches for common ground, and if you find none, you dislike the person. Strangely enough, what you find so repulsive about a person might just be a similarity to your own behaviour that you are not ready to face about yourself. And yet, the programming is simple—recognize who you think you are in others, and open up to those who match the profile. This is the difference between an enemy and a friend. A friend is someone you have many things in common with and an enemy is someone who is completely different. The heart feels what the mind directs it to feel.

Imagine if, instead of searching for similarities of experience or attitude, you acknowledged your existing connection with every person you met. Imagine if you recognized each person, each animal, each sunset, each moment as an indivisible part of yourself. Then, you would find love with everyone you met. Then, you would fall in love with every moment of your life.

Imagine how much freedom this would give you with other people. If you are free to love people whom you disagree with and people who disagree with you, people whose experiences are familiar and people whose experiences are alien—imagine how much you can learn about others. Imagine if you stopped judging people and fearing their judgment, and instead, recognized yourselves as existing within the unified fabric of love. Imagine how much you could see, how much you could understand, without being bound by the pressure to belong, because you know you already do.

Think of how much misunderstanding and isolation this simple difference generates. Most of us do not acknowledge love when we interact with people. We set up a thousand conditions against it. We run love through a hundred tests before we allow ourselves to consider the possibility of it. On a date, for example, the mind will search for someone with the same interests, opinions, goals. It will search for someone in the same mood, with the same body language, the same gestures. The focal point of comparison is the self. We think we like people for who they are, but we only like them for how much we think they represent our own selves. What a limited way to examine the world.

We walk away from an interaction thinking "what a wonderful person" because she has mirrored our conscious self-concept. Then, when the bliss of the trigger fades, we want to see her again. We become addicted to people, substances, situations, and words. Love is the ultimate drug. The desire to experience the state of love awareness hides behind each and every addiction. It is behind our greed, lust, envy, and gluttony. We tend to believe that we want that thing or that person, but really we're seeking that feeling of harmony. We want to feel like we're part of the whole. We want to remember ourselves.

It is not that all triggers are harmful. What can be harmful about a piece of soothing music or a beautiful sunset? These are triggers too. What is harmful is the belief that triggers carry feelings inside of them. This is what makes us addicted and desperate. If we acknowledge our triggers as facilitators of a state of being that is always accessible to us, then we will not only allow the potency of these triggers to fade—we will expect it. Better yet, we will develop ways of thinking that allow us to remember love without having anyone or anything to remind us of it. It is only because we seek love as if it lives outside of ourselves that we miss it, again and again. If we can understand that love is already there, we can break free of our patterns of slavery to circumstance. We can take hold of feeding our own love hunger, just like we take hold of feeding our hunger for food, water, and air. We can stop being dependent, stop being addicted, and learn to make love sustainable.

5

FEEDING THE MIND

My greatest challenge has been to change the Mindset of people. Mindsets play strange tricks on us. We see things the way our minds have instructed our eyes to see.

MUHAMMAD YUNUS

When it comes to health, most of us think of diet and exercise. We believe that health is a matter of the body. When we speak of physical health, images arise of treadmills, apples, and measuring tapes around waists. Our conception of mental health is nothing like this. When we speak of mental health, images arise of doctor's offices, psychiatric hospitals, and medication bottles. While physical health is linked to aspects of wellness, mental health is linked to aspects of sickness. If asked about physical health, people are more or less comfortable revealing their relationship to healthy or unhealthy habits. If asked about mental health, most people respond with ignorance.

And who could blame us? When do we learn to have a healthy mind or to care for a sick one? In dealing with mental health issues, stories of spontaneous recovery or self-guided healing are rare. A more common story is of treating symptoms, reducing the pain of suffering while keeping it alive, often for a lifetime. We pour fertilizer over the orchard—and there is nothing wrong with fertilizer—but we forget about the simple things. We forget about love.

When it comes to our bodies, we tend to believe that we are what we eat. We know that, if we eat junk food, our bodies will feel like junk. There may be some dispute about taste, but there is no dispute about the fact that healthy food makes you healthy. This, precisely, is how the mind works too. The mind, just like the body, becomes exactly what it is fed. While the body is nourished by food, the mind is nourished by thoughts. Our thoughts go on to trigger certain emotions, which then trigger certain behaviours. Most mental health interventions come between the thought and the feeling, or between the feeling and the action. Doctors prescribe pills to stop the thought from triggering the feeling, or they teach the patient skills to stop acting on his impulses. Sometimes it works, sometimes it doesn't. The thoughts, however, still persist. More often than not, the suffering person is doomed to either medicate or wilfully resist his compulsions for life, never quite free of what ails him.

Thoughts are what we pour onto the roots of our minds. When we pour fresh water onto a flower's roots, we make the plant healthy and its leaves naturally open to receive the sun. The more you feed your mind the healthy thoughts it needs, the stronger you become and the more you open to love. If, however, you water your roots with tar, the leaves will shrivel and the sun will not enter. Just like your body naturally responds positively to some foods, your mind naturally responds positively to some thoughts. We write off our suffering as incurable, while we believe all our thoughts to be true and anaesthetize the pain of our suffering. We sell ourselves short. The solution to healing ourselves does not lie in blindly numbing our emotions, but rather in listening to them and using the pain as a signal to shift our awareness.

For the average person, her thoughts are muted. They float inside her head, day after day, drifting in and out, triggering emotion after emotion, but she does not hear the thoughts themselves. The thoughts simply act as guides. Both closing the mind and opening the mind, though they have such drastically different effects, are processes that use the same fuel. Just like the same lever can be used to open a curtain or close it, so the mind can be opened or closed with thoughts. The mind is like a gateway. If we use the keys to open the gate, it is simply something we pass by on our way to the feast. If, however, we use the keys to lock the gate, the gateway becomes a roadblock. Like this, the mind breeds suffering.

Our thoughts direct our attention and, thus, they change our perception and our experience. On the path of love, thoughts are the torches that either light our path home or stray us into the woods. When we are on the path, we feel comfortable. When we are lost, we feel panic. Most of us have shame about our emotions, but feelings are just communication signals between mind and body. If you ate nails, your stomach would hurt, and it's a good thing that it would. Eating nails is deadly, thus the pain is helpful. Like this, sadness, anger, and anxiety are not to be feared or shamed, but listened to and decoded. Like rotten fruits on a tree, unpleasant emotions tell us that there is something wrong. A pain in the heart should be taken just like a pain in the gut—like the result of having consumed something awful.

Perhaps the most liberating moment of my life was when I realized that my self-loathing was not a product of my inadequacy but, rather, a product of my thoughts. For most of my life, I would look at myself and think that I was ugly, fat, unwanted, hideous, and a multitude of other adjectives. These thoughts would make me feel a horrible, sinking feeling in my chest. Then, more thoughts would come. My attention would focus only on the parts of my environment that acted as evidence for my thoughts. I would erase and warp giant parts of reality simply to find proof that I was, in fact, a hideous, disgusting freak. When my partner did not seem interested in me, I would ascribe it immediately to my physical inadequacy. I would completely miss the fact that he had been working all day and was preparing for bed. All I saw was what my thoughts had instructed my eyes to see.

Thoughts that block our perception of love make us feel trapped, frustrated, and angry. Having locked ourselves out of the feast, we stand outside the iron gates, starving and cold. Deprived of nourishment, we don't ask how we can enter. Instead, we question our own worth. Do I deserve love? If I can't get in, if I can't seem to get that feeling, maybe that means I don't deserve it. Maybe I'm not good enough to be loved. All the while, the keys lie in our pockets, ready to open the gate at any time. However, our thoughts about our thoughts keep us from taking the right action. This means that, until the suffering person realizes that the cause of her suffering and the answer to her salvation lies in her mind, she can do nothing. After she realizes this, however, she will find what she needs—the only medicine that can cure the lovesick.

*

Some thoughts come and go. Other thoughts linger for a few hours and disappear. Then, there are the thoughts that stick. They make a home inside our minds and develop into constant states of awareness. In these states, we are no longer conscious of our thoughts; we just act on them. We accept our thoughts as true. This state of constant awareness, the mindset, is beyond just a belief. It is an automatic, auto-pilot state of mind. Every mindset naturally sets the stage for its own correlated set of feelings and actions. With our minds set on some "truth," we lose conscious awareness of our mental patterns. We program our GPS and then we go for the ride.

To find out how thoughts turn into mindsets, we need only ask: whom do our thoughts answer to? If the mind is a system of government and all thoughts are potential leaders—who chooses the leaders? The answer lies in the heart. Our emotions are like the public who vote on the candidates in an election. Our feelings, just like the citizens, want to feel more security, connection, and happiness. They want less fear, pain, and isolation. In the end, it is not the candidate's intent, character, or goals that sway the public. It is the candidate's ability to prove to the public that he, above all others, holds the most promise in helping them pursue joy and avoid pain. This, too, is how we choose our thoughts. Ideally, we would only have thoughts that make us happy. However, a mind, like a system of government, does not function by ideals.

Just like your mind's gates close to love, people find themselves as citizens in dictatorships. They become trapped and limited by the very authorities they once chose and trusted. Historically and metaphorically, happy people do not elect or support dictators. It is only in times of crisis that people become completely irrational. If some emergency situation arises that makes the citizens feel stressed, fearful, or vigilant, they will have little power to make sound, logical choices. If asked to vote, they will vote for whoever promises them safety. It does not matter if the candidate is lying. If he tells them that, by choosing him, they will never, ever have to suffer like they've suffered, they'll go along obediently. In times of crisis, we just want to feel safe and we will accept even the most unreasonable "truth" to access that safety.

After the dictator comes into power, over time, patterns start to emerge that confuse the public. They're not sure they feel comfortable with what is happening, but they don't feel they have a choice. After all, he made all those promises and he says he knows what he's doing. Who are they not to trust him? Who are they to question him? Some of the greatest atrocities of our time have happened in such a pattern. The most inhumane systems have arisen out of people choosing leadership in times of crisis. By this same pattern, we have chosen the thoughts that lead our minds. Post-crisis, a person can live in a mind of tyranny, complete with self-loathing, anxiety, anger, and fear. However, she doesn't break out of those cycles because, after all, all those worries and rituals are supposed to keep her safe. Right?

A closed mind is a sign of tyrannical thoughts that continue to keep it closed. Thoughts of fear, inadequacy, and ridicule prevail within, blocking any possibility for love awareness. For some people, their only moments of peace are in states of intoxication. Those with the most closed minds purchase love, demand love, force love. They live isolated from the world, like walking dead, leaving a path of pain, struggle, and misery every-where they go. Their oppressive thoughts have turned into an oppressive mindset. Their mind functions automatically and effortlessly to keep them hurt, isolated, and resentful. They do not mean to harm, just like soldiers do not mean to harm. We are all prone to doing horrible things under the wrong authority. A mind gone astray from its true nature, from love and compassion, is a mind that needs new leadership, new thoughts.

The mind, in resetting to love, may undergo a revolution. However, as we've learned from history, violent revolutions often lead to a future of violence. They cause one oppressive regime to replace another. The answer to solving issues of government, including mind government, does not lie in resisting that which is oppressive. Like Carl Jung taught us: "What you resist, persists." To cultivate a love mindset, you need not actively cleanse your mind of all the self-protective, self-loathing, judgmental thoughts. Like a tree watered with vodka, a mind polluted with these thoughts has already faced the consequences. The branches and leaves have already suffered. There is no way to take this back.

The solution is not to reverse the past or to remove the damage. It is, simply, to move forward into the future, taking every opportunity to feed the roots fresh, cold water. The same way that a tiny thought in our childhood can manifest, thirty years later, as an anxiety disorder, one tiny thought right now can manifest just six months from now as unconditional love and unshakable happiness. Everything starts with a thought. It is not a complicated process. It is simple. We feed the mind thoughts of unity, harmony, and interconnectedness, and the mind develops awareness. Over time, it becomes easy to live without struggling and love without hesitating.

Thoughts of harmony allow experiences of harmony. The most interesting thing I have discovered on this journey is that people who have always had a love mindset may not understand the concept. They may not identify as spiritual. They may not be particularly interested in the concepts of love or unity by name. In their actions and attitudes, however, there is the presumption of universal equality. These people have been fed loving thoughts about themselves and others since birth, so they live in love naturally. Their love mindset is so automatic, so well-functioning, that they do not even hear the thoughts that keep their minds open. The gates stand, and have always stood, ajar, ready to receive the loving experience. This state of effortless, easy, and constant love is accessible for anyone and everyone who is willing to use the keys in his pocket to open, rather than shut, the gates that lead to love. Whether we are working on becoming anxious or becoming loving, everything takes practice, and everything starts with one thought.

*

Feeding the mind is simple, but I cannot call it easy. Simplicity is a structure. Most things that are true are simple. To lose weight, eat less than you burn. To understand people, listen. To develop confidence, take action. To stop worrying, let go. To become joyful, do things you love. These are simple in that they are complete concepts that take no more than a sentence to say. They are not, however, easy, because they must be applied consistently. This takes effort, thus many people say that it is difficult, perhaps too difficult to undertake. In Western society, we are encouraged to seek the ease of comfort rather than suffer the perceived difficulty of change. We are sold on magic cures and one-step solutions. We set resolutions and break them. We summon up willpower and then we cave to old patterns. We yo-yo diet, not only with food, but with love and self-care.

The truth is that no matter how difficult it is to secure a positive change, avoiding it is much more difficult in the long run. Living a life without love is, without a doubt, the most difficult thing to do. Think of the difference between the endless, helpless pain from a lifetime of short-term, self-defeating, yo-yo failures compared to the temporary pain of creating sustainable habits of responding that will serve you in the long term.

A person with a love mindset is like a tree in an orchard that gets the perfect amount of sunlight and rain. It is may not be easy to set up an orchard this way, but it will be the easiest kind of orchard to maintain. That which is good for us requires less upkeep than that which is not. Living in a mind polluted with isolating, self-defeating thoughts is incredibly difficult. It is like drowning. To suffer in an unloving mind is to spend your life breathlessly, helplessly underwater. Once in a while, you surface up and take a gulp of air. You remember that, maybe, you don't have to suffer anymore. Whether it's by your own realization or helped by some guru, you have moments of hope when you realize that, maybe, it doesn't have to be so hard. Without a mindset change, however, you plunge right back into those thoughts. When you aren't blindly self-destructing, you alternate between "I can't live like this" and "Maybe I don't have to." The only moments of happiness are those little moments of hope and clarity. In such a state, all love awareness is accidentally triggered and soon lost. This is the most difficult way to live.

Living with the love mindset is the opposite. Your default setting is with lungs full of fresh air. Even when you plunge back into toxic thinking, you recognize that something unhealthy is happening. Your normal state is breathing, and your crisis state is drowning. Living like this, there are also moments of sudden realization. You will remember all those years when drowning was your "normal" and air was a rare gift. Filled with the power of love, you will look back at these memories, thinking "How could I ever have lived like that?" Perhaps this will fuel your desire to help others who have never lived with their heads above water—who may not believe that such a thing is possible.

Changing the thoughts that you feed your mind is just like changing the foods that you feed your body. Like any adjustment to a better way of life, purpose fuels the journey. When I truly desire something, nothing can stop me. When I believe that something is completely possible and direly necessary to my existence, I will find a way to do it, use it, execute it. We make time to sleep, because we accept that we need it. So it goes with feeding the mind. Of course, you must remember to feed it, like you'd feed a child until the child learns to feed herself. Most people back away from transforming their minds because they believe that it's difficult. We have been mass conditioned to believe that building good habits is difficult while building bad habits is easy. To see through this veil of ignorance, you need only ask yourself how difficult it is to starve and, by comparison, how difficult it is to learn to cook.

6

YOU AND I

We are never more discontented with others than when we are discontented with ourselves.

HENRI FREDERIC AMIEL

I used to think that other people could hurt me. I used to think, also, that other people could save me. Alone with my own self, life was unbearable. There was always an inner voice screaming at me about my ugly body, my lack of charisma, my inadequacy as a female, as a daughter, as a human being. I found a few ways to drown the voice out. Every all-consuming self-modification project, such as a diet for example, consumed so much mind energy that I was distracted from my plight. Over time, however, the distraction factor would fade and I would respond by distracting even harder. And thus, the diet turned into an eating disorder. I followed this same process over and over, each time hoping that my new endeavour would be my final one; yet nothing would last. Time after time, the critic within would return. The longer the voices stayed absent, the more intensely they would return. Over this process, I felt no control.

About my relationship with myself, I had no insight or understanding. I just walked through life in fear of the tyranny that came from the inside of my head. The biggest problem was that I didn't know it came from my own head. I thought that other people were causing me pain, when they were just accidentally clicking "play" on already existing tapes inside my mind. My relationships with others became defined by their ability either to save me from my misery or to hurt me by perpetuating it. Everyone was either a prince or an attacker. I had to be the victim or the princess, the worshipped or the abandoned.

One day, the excruciating, unbearable pain of my suffering was interrupted. With my first ever lover, I found a treatment for my sorrow. His words and deeds brought me sensations I'd never felt before. He told me I was beautiful and interesting. He paid attention when I spoke and he missed me when I was gone. At first, I was in pure ecstasy. Soon enough, I was hooked. Next to him, everything else took second place. Nothing else mattered. There was only me, him, and that feeling of cosmic connection. He was my gateway. He was my entry ticket into eternity. Around him, there was no longer any pain. There was only the pleasure of feeling completely and utterly alive, connected, and accepted. We would lie together, embracing, and I would feel our bodies merging together as my skin washed top to bottom with utter bliss.

As for my pain, I thought it was all done with. Almost a year into our relationship, after I'd shared with him the intimate stories of my life to date, he said to me words I have never forgotten.

"People have treated you badly in the past," he said, stroking my hair and embracing me. "I'm going to do better. I'm going to treat you better."

I remember thinking, right then and there, that it was the happiest moment of my life. And, for a long time, it really was. Another year later, my heaven remained. I was convinced that the darkness had been vanquished and that he had been my saviour. I thought I'd found the Prince Charming that most women could only dream about.

After one more year, the fairy tale showed its true face. Soon enough, we grew up and moved in together. Real life took over. He worked long hours and I went to school. He wasn't home very often and I spent many nights with myself. Without him there, I was alone with my mind—my self-loathing, judgmental mind. The thing about hating myself was that I didn't realize that I was doing it. I didn't know that everyone else didn't talk to themselves like I did. I didn't even realize that I was talking to myself in any particular way. All I felt was the same old misery, the same old suffering. The moments without him became pure torture and, in my mind, it was all his fault.

"You don't love me; you told me you'd do better," I would hiss through tears and anger.

That really stung. He'd promised to do better and, now, he wasn't. The more I blamed him, the more he fought back. He started drinking heavily. He started spending even less time at home. When he did come, our arguments escalated into some of the most violent confrontations of my life. I left him, indignant and bitter, feeling like I deserved better, like I'd been done wrong once again.

I entered my next relationship full of horror stories about my last one. He, too, promised me to do better. For a while, it was great, though definitely less powerful. By then, I was already somewhat guarded. This whole love thing, I thought, wasn't what it seemed. It was a beautiful rose complete with hidden thorns. Nevertheless, I believed the promises and, for a while, the pain abated. Within just six months, it returned full force.

That same pattern continued to happen, not just in my romantic relationships, but in my hobbies, friendships, and jobs. At first, the novelty would dull the pain, but soon enough the same old darkness would return. I'd blame it on other people and circumstances, on my partner and the weather, on the time of day and the horrors of my past.

I drove myself deeper and deeper into the darkness. I did things that made it harder and harder for me to face my own reflection. Eventually, I didn't face her at all. I lost all sense of morality and conscience. When I finally broke down, I broke down alone, having pushed everyone else away. In the gloomiest depth of my breakdown, I saw clearly who was bringing me all of my pain, all of my suffering. I saw who didn't love me. I realized, with razor-sharp clarity, who really needed to do better. Looking into my own eyes in the mirror, I greeted myself. It was like looking at an enemy. The eyes stared back, distant and hostile.

"People have treated you badly in the past," I whispered slowly to the girl in the mirror, "and I'm going to do better. I'm going to treat you better."

Her eyes softened and filled with tears. My enemy turned into a friend.

*

Your own self is your most trusted frame of reference for the rest of the world. Whatever you think of yourself, you will think of every person, thing, and event in the universe. Sometimes, this is a direct translation: I am depressed, so the world is depressing. Other times, it is a bit more complex: I am worthless, so other people are more worthy. These appear to be opposites, yet there is a common frame of reference—the assumption that some people have more worth than others. If we were to be absolutely accurate, we would always start sentences with "I" and never "You," "We," or "They." "I," however, hides behind the other pronouns. The "I" conceals itself in the roots of mindset, while the outward behaviours, opinions, and emotions seem to react only to the outside world.

Your relationship to yourself, then, is and always will be directly reflected in all your relationships with others. If you do not know how to appreciate yourself as a piece of nature, how could you appreciate others this way? Of course, there are those who claim that they do love other people without loving themselves, because they give so much to others. But how can we have an awareness of someone else as a beautiful, interconnected part of ourselves without having an awareness of ourselves as the same? Like this, we believe we love others or that we give to them unconditionally, when really we are fostering co-dependence and reinforcing our poor self-concepts through unsustainable relationships. We believe we see reality, that we see other people, but we see only as far as our self-imposed limits.

Our thoughts, whether they are conscious or unconscious, direct our awareness and elicit feelings. When we experience a thought about ourselves such as "I am not good enough," it directs our awareness either towards minute parts of reality or towards a distorted reality. From that limited focus, we start to feel shame. These cycles do not stop at self-perception. Compared to a rock or a tiger, our neighbour is our identical match. Thus, our tyrannical thoughts do not stop within the confines of our self-evaluation. He who judges himself will always judge others. She who does not understand herself will always misunderstand others. The rubric we develop for ourselves, the measuring stick we put against our own mind and body, generalizes to every other human being. The more distorted our view of self is, the more distorted will be our view of everything and everyone around us.

The thoughts that we feed to our own roots are like the contents of our own personal watering can. If we've got poison in the can, then that's what we'll use on ourselves and that's what we'll use on others. If we could find a way to sustainably get water, of course we'd throw the poison away. We nourish either no one or everyone. Thus, we only treat other people as well as we treat ourselves. Those who have hurt us, too, have given themselves the same dose of harm. The harshest, cruellest, meanest deeds you've ever incurred have come from someone who's received just the same and who would give himself just the same. However someone has spoken to you in a time of anger is surely how she also speaks to herself in her darkest moments. We water one another's roots with whatever we give to ourselves. We deny the same love to others that we deny ourselves. We distort others in the same way we distort ourselves.

The source of our incompetence in watering our own roots lies in our depending on others to do so. The greatest barrier to self-love and to cultivating a love mindset is our waiting for other people to "give" us love—our addiction to triggers. This is exactly what my first lover was: an addiction. It was not he, as a living, breathing person, who made me swoon. Rather, it was the effect that he had on me. He opened my mind to thoughts like "I am beautiful" and "I am interesting." From that, I overflowed with joy. He watered my mind for me, which kept me from needing to water it myself. While he was there, I was well fed. When he left, I starved.

This is how most relationships function. When we first meet a person, especially a love interest, we build momentum as we project ourselves onto one another. I like you and you like me. Your being around me triggers my love awareness and makes me feel good about myself, which makes me feel closer to you. You make me feel beautiful and so I want to make you feel beautiful. You make me feel worthy and respected, so I want to make you feel the same. When I do, you feel better about yourself, so you trigger me back. This sort of up-wards moving cycle can go on for years—feeding one another, watering each other's minds with loving words and much needed triggers.

This same momentum can bring us back down. You ignored me today. That made me feel bad about myself. So, I ignored you right back. I make you feel as bad as I feel. Perhaps you were just tired, but now, my ignoring you has made you feel inadequate. So, you hurt me back. And on-wards we go. When we do not control our relationship with ourselves, the relationship is con-trolled by involuntary triggers. We then become helpless dancers in the tango of mutual destruction. If you've been in it, you know how far down it goes. The longer we dance, the more we deprive each other. We are so busy blaming one another for our hunger that we forget the simple solution. We forget to feed ourselves.

In this way, most so-called love relationships are really just addictions. They are just refuges away from our own starvation and escapes from our own responsibilities to our own minds, to our own destinies. Romantic relationships are the supposed solutions to all our problems, but, for most people, they just precipitate the pain. The only thing worse than having thoughts of being unworthy is having someone else tell you that you're unworthy. This feeling is so awful that the only thing the desperate lover can think to do is to make her lover feel unworthy right back. We so deeply crave to be on the same level that, when we cannot bring ourselves up to someone's happiness, we will try to drag him down into our misery. This is how love hunger spreads in families. This is how self-loathing parents breed self-loathing children who get into relationships with other self-loathing people. Love hunger is an epidemic perpetuated by our lack of awareness about ourselves. We reach out for love as if it lies somewhere outside of us. We look for relationships with others as if they can repair our relationships with ourselves.

In truth, people know very little about each other. I only know as much about you as I know about myself. I only accept your mistakes and flaws to the degree that I accept my own. I only perceive you to be giving to me that which I would give to myself. I only read, in your words, the meaning which I would draw out of my own words spoken in such a fashion. I only ascribe to your facial expressions, body language, and behaviour the same meanings that I would ascribe to mine. I only give you as much as I think I deserve to get. I only praise you as much as I think I deserve to be praised. I only love you as much as I think I deserve to be loved.

For me, self-loathing was a permanent state of mind. It was my mindset. I was completely focused on feeding poison, and only poison, into the roots of my mind. Of course, when others came along with water, I accepted it hungrily, but this did not last after they were gone. In the presence of a lover, I felt beautiful and worthy. When they left, the same old thoughts would return. I fed myself what I was used to feeding myself. As long as the person in front of me could trigger me into a more loving relationship with myself, they were safe. If, however, they were busy, tired, or just in a bad mood—they were not safe. They received the same treatment as I gave myself. Then, they'd shoot right back.

It used to be that every "You" in my life was a source of pain. I know now that the source, the origin of all that pain was not "You," it was me. The people around me were just people with their own suffering. They hoped to be distracted from their feelings of shame by my presence. When things turned sour, we'd both walk away feeling wronged and resentful. With every failed relationship, my victim theory would gain strength. Every interaction soon became a self-fulfilling prophecy. I expected them to do to me what I'd done to myself. I expected them to think of me as ugly and useless, to break my trust and my heart, to love me for a little while and then get sick of me. I got everything I thought I deserved. Every "You" gave me exactly what I thought they would.

Most people live in a world of what they think are other people, but are really just their own selves imprinted on seven billion faces. As Anaïs Nin said, "We don't see things as they are, we see them as we are." Any change in perception of others is only temporary in the absence of a change in perception about self. The shelves of the bookstores are lined with advice about marriage, romance, and long-term commitment. There are lists, checklists, and practical guides. These are all well and good, but if our most long-standing relationship with our best known human is not in good shape, no lists or guides will help. Isolation from self is isolation from everyone else. As long as self-love is temporary, induced only by environmental triggers, then all relationships and all happiness will be temporary as well. Thus, the love mindset starts at home. It starts with your relationship with yourself. All love begins with the love within.

7

WHO YOU REALLY ARE

Self is the only prison that can ever bind the soul.

HENRY VAN DYKE

The oldest cliché in the book is that to love anyone, you must first love yourself. We live in the age of self-esteem, self-confidence, and self-love. Everyone from your psychotherapist to the beauty magazine encourages you to "love yourself" without much further guidance. Recently, I saw a headline that said something to the effect of: "Go ahead; give yourself some love and laser off those moles once and for all." The self-love movement has become, at best, misguided.

So what does it really mean to love yourself? To love yourself is to love your true self, your authentic self. Unfortunately, like "love yourself," the messages of "be yourself" and "stay true to who you are" have become so popular that they have lost meaning. These phrases materialize in motivational paraphernalia so frequently that they have grown bland and hardly anyone bothers to explain what they really stand for anymore.

One particularly troublesome way that people define "who you are" is by drawing on this idea of a fixed, unique destiny. To find yourself is to find your own special, individual self. Common rhetoric about self-discovery teaches that the search for yourself is the search for your innate and unchanging preferences, strengths, and talents. It is a quest for what you *are* as opposed to what you are *not*. As in, I am a baseball player, not a banker. I am an introvert, not an extrovert. I am a chef, not a pilot. I am business-minded, not artistic. And so on.

This model of the inner self suggests a beautiful idea—that each of us has his or her own special place in the world. If we discover what that place is, we will be happy forever because we'll be living out our destiny. Destiny is something predetermined so, when we set ourselves to fulfilling it, we become part of a larger, more intelligent mechanism. We look at people that we have decided to remember in our history books and it seems clear that they all had a destiny. How could da Vinci not have painted? How could Mozart not have composed? Surely, there was an inner painter in one and an inner musician in the other. The inspirational message of the static authentic self is that, if you look deeply enough inside yourself, you will find your inner substance, which is different from the inner substance of others. If you do this, then you have the chance to discover your own greatness—your own chance to slide into the history books. Unfortunately, neither the beauty of the idea nor the comfort of hope that it instills strikes out the corollary anxiety, fear, and doubt which inevitably accompany this type of thinking.

The problem lies in thinking that we must find some predetermined outcome as opposed to creating it. Fate robs us of choice, responsibility, and power. This does not only apply to finding the true self. The idea of the predetermined, unique, authentic self is strikingly similar to the idea of the soul mate. While the programmed inner self represents personal destiny, the soul mate represents romantic destiny. The authentic self is who you're meant to *be* and the soul mate is who you're meant to be *with*. Both destinies imply affinity. The authentic self supposedly has a natural affinity for certain skills and environments. Soul mates supposedly have a natural affinity for one another in terms of sex, intellect, and emotion.

Both types of destiny also imply selectivity. The authentic self is supposed to have an affinity only for certain activities and not others. The true self, then, is only as valuable as its exposure to the work at which it excels. The soul mate is the ultimate form of selectivity. If there is just one person with whom we can have a natural affinity, this presupposes that there are seven billion people with whom we do not. The heart of the soul mate is only as valuable as its exposure to its predestined match. These models of personal growth and building relationships are more harmful than they are beneficial. These ideas easily lead to fear of commitment, choice paralysis, and chronic self-doubt.

The seeker of the authentic self struggles to find her true calling before it's too late. She, like all other people, has gathered joy from more than just one kind of activity. How can she decide? If she loves playing music, painting, and medicine, how can she choose which one is her true destiny? She feels that there is one correct choice; she has one true calling. The commitment to this choice is so great that she will spend as long as possible avoiding it. She may become so paralyzed by choice that she may not choose at all. She may find it easier to move into work that gives her no joy rather than mistakenly pursue a wrongful destiny. Misguided hope can appear a bigger danger than wilful ignorance. If she does choose, she may be satisfied for a while. However, every time she runs into a period of difficulty, conflict, or stagnation, she'll inevitably wonder whether she chose correctly. When we base our life satisfaction on the static inner self, we base our lifelong happiness upon a single choice. Then, we spend our lives questioning that choice. Ironically, she who believes in personal destiny will find herself less capable of fulfilling it.

Likewise, he who believes in soul mates carries the burden of finding and choosing the perfect mate. The process of selection is the most important part of the relationship. He tries to decode the subtleties of body language and tongue, personal history and word choice, sense of humour and colour of hair. He creates a mental idea of perfection to which he compares each candidate. Finding no one who is as perfect as the illusion in his head, he will either avoid commitment while searching evermore for his faultless illusion, or he will choose a real person in the interim. If he chooses to commit to anyone, he will be plagued by the idea that he settled. Even if things sail smoothly for the first while, conflict will tear the relationship apart. Time away from one another will create distance. He will leave her to find his perfect match. And why wouldn't he? If there is someone out there to whom he is better suited, why wouldn't he leave? He who believes in soul mates never ceases to doubt if his current partner is, truly, "The One." As a result, the great irony emerges: those who believe in soul mates are much less likely to actually find one.

*

Of all thoughts that we've ever experienced, the "I" thought has been, by far, the most long-standing and the most influential on our mindset. Of all the roots that we have, the root of our own identity burrows the deepest. It all started with the first "I am" thought. "I am Vironika." "I am Peter." It all begins innocently with just a name. As we grow, the thought strengthens. "I really am Vironika!" The thought gives me comfort. I know that this is who I am. Each time I am called this, I respond, and there is someone waiting to attend to me. I feel safe knowing that I am Vironika and not something or someone else. The comfort of identity is our first solidifying belief.

Over time, other "I" thoughts get fed to our roots and we soak them up readily. When we're children, we soak up anything and everything we're given. If I am told that I am a girl and, because of that, I like dolls, then I will say I like dolls. If I am told that I am not good at sports, then I'll say I am not good at sports. I trust others to tell me who I am. I also desperately *want* to know who I am. I want to formulate a permanent identity, a core self. I deeply desire to have certainty about myself. In this desire, I take whatever I'm given without discriminating whether or not it is true. I have no idea what is true and what is not. I just eat the thoughts, all the "You are" statements, and turn them into "I am" statements. These gather and, over time, I use them as my identity.

If, somehow, my experiences give me feedback that is different from I am told to receive—if I hate dolls or enjoy sports, for example—then I am faced with an identity crisis. This can happen when we are 5, 25, or 85. An identity crisis happens when our self-definitions and our experiences collide, causing our self-concept to come under the harsh light of awareness. We are forced to examine and alter our identity. Sometimes, the alteration seems harmless, helpful even. Maybe I stop identifying as being bad at sports, and start identifying myself as athletic. Other times, it is obviously toxic. Maybe I stop identifying as one of the pretty, desirable girls and start identifying as a weird, unlovable freak. Both changes of identity would explain the rift between my thoughts and my experiences.

We face this crisis when we begin school, transitioning from pleasing only our parents to needing to impress a whole peer group. Who must I be if people are going to like me? Who am I if people don't like me? We face this crisis when siblings are born and when we move to new places. We face it when we find differences between our preferences and what we are taught is "normal." We face it when we experience trauma, disease, failure. We face it when major relationships dissolve. Who am I if I am not your partner anymore? Now, I must find out who I am apart from who I was with you. This happens to us in times of healing, recovery, and catastrophe. Most of us have had dozens of identity crises throughout our lives.

Sometimes, an identity crisis is triggered without our desire or involvement, such as the death of a relative. Other times, it is triggered by our own efforts, such as choosing to quit smoking. In both cases, our awareness jolts out of automatic functioning. When our behavioural or environmental routines are interrupted, our mind is interrupted also. Our thoughts are cruising on autopilot, when suddenly, we remember that there's a switchboard.

Take a moment to remember the identity crises that you've experienced in your life. When have you looked at yourself, literally or figuratively, and thought—what does this mean about who I am? Why did this happen to me, and not to others? Was it my fault? Am I doing the right thing? What do I want? Is what I've been doing important to me? What *is* important to me? Am I the kind of person who can do what I want to do? Why am I here? What am I capable of?

Questions about identity are often painful. The mind is directing us effortlessly in some direction and, suddenly, we're shocked by the sudden loss of certainty. It's like driving somewhere for four hours and suddenly realizing that you've gone north when you should have gone south. Except it hasn't been four hours—it's been a quarter or half a century. Identity questions often arouse feelings of regret, shame, anxiety, panic, guilt, and helplessness. For this reason, most people either ignore the questions or they segue immediately into some new identity. Over time, we become more efficient at repressing and replacing—we rush to act before we can panic. We grow accustomed to our cycles of losing and gaining self-understanding. After all, one can get used to anything—even dying.

These moments of self-questioning, however, are prime opportunities to discover the love mindset. These are times when, instead of ignoring our confusion or switching from one invented identity to another, we can take a good look at ourselves and find out, once and for all, who we really are.

*

We all have two identities. The first is the core identity. This is the authentic self, spirit, soul, inner self, true self, and all its other names. The second is the surface identity. This is the external self. It includes absolutely everything else, including your personality, character, body, words, and behaviour.

The difference between the two selves is that one is permanent and one is impermanent. One changes and one does not. The difference is simple. The difficulty that most people face, however, is in classification. They assume permanence where it does not exist and call impermanent that which is always present. In this process, we lose ourselves. Just like we lose love by assuming that it can be gained or lost, we lose self-love by assuming our temporary self to be permanent.

The external self is like a tree. The tree can die and will die. It is not permanent. There are parts of the tree that are there for as long as the tree is there, but when the tree dies, they will die along with it. One such part is the inside of the trunk. As long as the tree lives, the inside of the trunk lives. There are other parts which are on the tree only occasionally, such as fruits, and other portions that become a part of the tree for only a short period of time, such as a nest. In any case, whether they are short-lived developments or long-term factions, all visible parts of the tree will, at one point, die. This is the external self. This is character, hair, and skill.

It is easy to make the mistake of identifying the longest standing parts of the external self as authentic. Though it may seem innocent enough, this is the most dangerous mistake. In it, we can find the source of much of our suffering. The danger of ascribing permanence to impermanent things is very clear when we look at something like depression or anxiety. If I say, "I am a depressed person," I presuppose my inability to rid myself of depression. It becomes a part of what I believe is my permanent identity, rather than a temporary state that exists and comes for a reason—as a communication mechanism. If I say, "I am weak," I ensure that I stay weak. If I say, "I cannot," "I'm not the type to," "I am not able," then I set up a self-fulfilling prophecy. As I think of myself, so I shall be. As I think of myself, so I shall think of others. Through my thoughts of myself, I will create my reality.

The problem is clear with negative labels. If I say that I am ugly, incompetent, or inadequate, I make myself miserable. However, positive labels can be harmful too. If I say that I am a golfer, for example, because I have been playing golf since I was a small child, this seems to be positive. Many personal development gurus would encourage you to identify with your passions and skills. What if, however, I get an injury that prevents me from ever playing golf again? Then, I suffer. I suffer just as much as the person who identifies as depressed. I have called myself something that I can no longer be. I have placed the secret key to my happiness within something that I can no longer have. I put the key to my joy into someone else's pocket and now they've run away, and I have nowhere to go but down.

Everything, except for the inner self, is impermanent. Accepting this is simply accepting the truth. Refusing this sets us up for pain and misery. It is common for people to expect permanence from the external self because we need certainty. We need to have a permanent core identity. There's a need in us for this just like there's a need in us to love each other. We have drives to get what we want, even when what we want is something that we already have. Thus, we seek for love and we seek for our true self. Both are already secure, permanent, and unchanging. We need not seek anywhere except inside ourselves.

Most people have never thought of the inner self. If they have, they've given it impermanent properties. They've given it preferences, talents, or skills—all impermanent. They've given it affinity, appearance, and desire—all impermanent. What, then, is permanent? What, within us, can never change? What cannot be altered? What cannot be different, no matter what? What lies inside of us that cannot die because it cannot be born? What is there about which we can be absolutely, completely certain?

A tree's permanent essence cannot be found exclusively in its branches, leaves, or trunk. After all, every tree was once a seed, which did not have any of those external attributes. The essence of a tree does not come from inside the seed either, since that seed splits and the shell disintegrates within the soil. There is something beyond the physical form of the tree, something unchanging. There is something beyond the visible tree which unites it with the soil, the air, and the person sitting in its shade. Something allows the tree to grow when we pour water onto it, while pouring water on a plastic replica does nothing.

Some people will call this a soul—something alive beyond the physical. Some people wonder whether there is such a thing as a soul, just like some people wonder if there is such a thing as love. The way we interpret certain words makes us think that, perhaps, they refer to something outside of our experience. "Soul" is just a word, and words are only as valuable as the meaning we give to them. If you say "soul" and, by that, you mean a ghost-like creature that moves out at the moment of death to inhabit something being born, then I don't believe in a soul. But if we can interpret the word "soul" to mean "life energy"—this, I can vouch for, and this can be easily experienced.

Think of this: if I stand over a patch of soil, which receives plenty of rainfall and sunlight, with a seed in one hand and a shovel in the other, intending to plant that seed, where does life begin? Will it begin when I put the seed into the ground? Will it begin when the seed splits? Will it begin after the seedling bursts upwards and becomes visible? Did it already begin when I set an intention to plant the seed? Or did it begin when I first thought of planting it? While the life cycle of a tree may be said to "begin" at some point, the potential for life exists in past, present, and future.

Before the tree is planted and long after the tree dies, there is pure potential. If some ingredients mix together in a certain way, this potential takes the form of a tree. The potential, however, cannot be traced to the seed, the shovel, or the soil. It cannot be splintered into time or space. The potential is energy. It is infinite and ever-present, invisible and powerful. It is a web that entangles all of existence. The visible living thing is simply a thriving vehicle for that life energy—the energy that I have called "love."

Such inner potential is alive within every single human being. We all have it. We all have the same amount of it, the same bountiful abundance of it. Your inner self and my inner self are the same. We have not grown up thinking this way because, after all, I'm an oak tree and you're a maple tree. Our external forms have confused us, but we forget that, at the core, we are pure life living within a temporary body. We are more than something that lives and dies. We are something permanent that sticks around after our bodies are long gone.

Whether you call it energy, love, or God—it does not matter. You can call it the laws of thermodynamics as easily as you can call it spiritual consciousness. However you've been conditioned to think of it, you already know that there is something inside you that has no end.

This potential is the core identity. It cannot be born or die. It cannot be changed or altered. It is not to be seen or packaged. It is just pure life, pure potential. This is the only permanent part. Everything else is impermanent. Thus, when we arrange the external self, we must arrange it around our inner self. The inner self will not change. Thus, we must accept it and then go on to create all that must be created, change all that must be changed. The external self thrives only when we accept the internal self as a permanent reality. This works for the tree too. The laws of life will continue to work as they work. A tree's potential for growth is not visible to the naked eye, but this potential and its nature must be obeyed in order for the external body to materialize in its healthiest form.

The external self, then, is an expression of inner potential. Whether we arrange our external form to express this potential or not—this does not alter the inner self. It does, however, alter the external self. If a tree does not receive sun, the sun does not die. It is the tree that dies. Likewise, if a person does not receive love, she wilts. Love is unaltered. Her capacity to love and be loved is unaltered. Our living or dying depends entirely on whether or not we, as impermanent beings, become vessels for the permanent. Our mental and physical health depends on whether or not we accept our true selves and base our external selves completely on that truth. If we do this, we flourish. If we do not, we perish. These are the rules of life.

If you were starving and you smelled food, your mouth would water, your body signalling to you that nourishment is close by. This is exactly why we love compliments that speak of bravery, strength, and significance. We feel good when we hear about how powerful we are because we are pure power. Our minds thirst for anything that reminds us of the deepest wisdom of the soul. We deeply hunger to remember that we are immortal, indestructible, unstoppable, and eternal. We hunger for it because it is our deepest truth.

8

SEARCHING FOR PERMANENCE

Perhaps home is not a place but simply an irrevocable condition.

JAMES BALDWIN

The widespread epidemic of love hunger has left us shameful, lonely, and separated from one another. Why, then, do we not stand up and find our way back into each other's arms? Back into our own arms? What is it that keeps us from searching for love the same way that we would search for food if we were hungry? The answer is deceptively simple: we accept our need for food, but we do not accept our need for love. We can easily admit that, without food, we die. We cannot easily admit that, without love, we die. We can say, without a shadow of a doubt, that food is a part of us. The foods that we put into our stomachs decide our overall health. Some people, of course, know this deeper than others, but overall we all have a hunch. We know that there is a way to nourish our bodies that will put them into peak shape. Some people deny their bodies this nourishment, but not because they are ignorant of what is required. They know they need fruits and vegetables. They accept the idea of proper nourishment as a permanent part of their human body, even though they may define themselves as unable or unwilling, for some reason, to adhere their behaviours to their body's needs.

Love is different. About love, we are silent. We do not talk about how badly we all need love or acknowledge this need in each other. In the Western world, there is no common agreement on how we should interact with one another in order to facilitate peace, joy, and happiness between all people. The average person believes that there are bad people out there who do not deserve love. He does not see love as vital nourishment, but more like a candy dessert: not necessary, but a treat. Then, he judges people as worthy or unworthy of the treat. Most of us are ignorant of our human needs, so we do not speak of them aloud. This is how we've come to be ashamed of them.

Now more than ever, we live in the age of individuality. We are encouraged, from the time that we are young, to cultivate a separate identity that is uniquely ours. We evaluate ourselves by our ability to distinguish ourselves from the rest. This so-called accomplishment is fleeting. It is temporary. It is wildly unsatisfying, but most people do not see a better way. I remember years ago being very upset when a close friend, who had already started listening to my favourite music and wearing my style of clothes, mentioned that she wanted to dye her hair the same colour as mine. In that moment, I felt rage. I felt a loss of identity. I thought, at the time, that my rage was towards her. I know now that my rage was only towards myself. In her actions, I recognized my own. I saw a girl trying to define her identity by her outward appearance, to adorn herself in the fashion of mass-produced individualism that is easily replicable by anyone with a credit card. My rage was only at myself.

Deep within, we have a desire for permanence. We have a love-shaped hole within us. We crave so deeply to know that there is something that is certain, unmoving, and absolute. We want, so desperately, to have a permanent home where we always feel safe and welcome. We crave a permanent identity, a permanent relationship. We want stability and assurance. We want it so badly that we seek it wherever we can. If the most certainty we ever experience is in knowing, for sure, that if we put x amount of drugs into our system, we will get feeling y, then that is how we'll meet our need. If the only consistent thing we can find about ourselves is our tendency to be depressed, then we'll identify with that. We want a home so badly that, in the absence of any other visible options, we will make misery our home.

At the same time, we feel this deep craving for love. We long to connect with others and with ourselves. This need, too, we meet in any way we can. If the only way we think we can come together with others is in meaningless sexual encounters, then we will do so. If the only way we've found to meet our need for unity is to join a hateful and violent cult, we'll do so. If the most connected we've ever felt with another person was in that brief moment of apology and regret after physical abuse, then we'll seek that abuse for the rest of our lives.

The love mindset unites two vital needs. It is not only about finding permanence, nor is it just about finding unity. It is about both. It is about finding a home within us to which we can always return. Then, we can find that home in the eyes of every lover, friend, and stranger. In some religions, they say this will happen after death. They promise that, if we follow all the rules, we'll go to a place of eternity, unity, safety, and peace. How wonderful that we do not have to wait until we expire to enjoy such a place. This place exists in all of our minds.

*

Self-improvement without self-love is like building a house upon sand. You can build and build, but it will always sink. When we have the foundation of self-knowledge, of knowing our true self, we feel a permanent sense of belonging. Then, comfort travels with us everywhere. Our house can be torn down by a tornado, but we will still feel at home. To seek permanence where permanence actually lies is the key to happiness and peace.

The permanent self is not something that most people have explored. When they do explore it, they find it to be strangely unfamiliar. We are so used to defining ourselves as something in particular that defining ourselves as something universal, united, and equal seems unnatural. After all, I have been taught that I am me and you are you. If the authentic me is just like the authentic you, I lose something. I lose all the certainty I ever had, because I put all my faith into the uncertain.

The way that most people seek identity is by trying to match their external self to some external image of the "perfect" self. The typical woman compares herself to media-generated images of the perfect woman, the perfect mother, the perfect wife. The man compares himself to images of the perfect male, the perfect son, the perfect father. Then, each works to reach those ideals. The average person seeks permanence between magazine covers and in-between commercial breaks.

Although this process is immensely harmful to our self-worth, and is largely responsible for the epidemic of shame and fear in our culture, it is actually full of potential. After all, most of us are already matching our impermanent selves to some apparently permanent entity. We are already trying to change things that we see as changeable to match criteria that we believe are unchangeable. This process is perfect. There's nothing wrong with this process. All that we need to do, in order to secure a lifetime of love, peace, and happiness, is to change the criteria, to change our idea of the "ideal."

What is ideal? When most people think of the ideal self, what comes to mind is some combination of attributes: successful, fit, attractive, wealthy, admired, influential, funny, accomplished, etc. When we strive for this type of ideal self, every failure results in a loss of self-respect. And why wouldn't it? If I calculate my worth by my ability to sustain some temporary illusion, then my self-worth disappears in the absence of certain behaviours, conditions, and abilities. Thus, my worth as a person is always changing based on what I have, what I do, how other people react to me, and so on.

This type of self-image hinders us from reaching our full potential. If our safest place, our home, is in a place where we feel that we are flawless, then why would we ever take any risk? To be courageous we must be willing to surrender that temporary perfection, even for a moment. If my self-worth is attached to my so-called perfection, why would I ever do anything that would put it into question?

Our collective seeking for the ideal self has perpetuated an epidemic of fear. One summer evening, I stumbled upon a music show on the beach. The sun was setting and the band's resonating blues drew me in front of their quaint stage. The band was excellent, more deserving of an amphitheatre than the sparse crowd that had gathered there that day. Around the dance floor sat a few dozen people of all ages and styles, all of them darting their eyes around to look at others, while they gently rocked their feet and tapped their fingers. Some had stood up and, in their eyes, there was a deep hunger. I could almost see them dreaming of breaking into dance. Yet, they waited. Dozens of people all looking around, waiting for someone else to start dancing, someone else to do what they all wanted to do. If the typical dance club did not serve alcohol, it would be full of terrified, paranoid people, all wanting to dance yet fearing to move.

Why are we so afraid? Such hesitation would be unheard of in the rest of the world. If they heard music, especially good music, they would surely dance. To do anything else would seem foolish. Why wouldn't they dance? And why would it matter who is the first person to dance? Even if a group is shy, just one person's courage will encourage others. To most of the world, this is obvious. To us, it isn't even news. It is esoteric knowledge.

The problem with our culture is that we do not have a permanent sense of identity, so going out there and courageously dancing, singing, or otherwise putting ourselves out there holds a real risk for our self-worth. We have found safety in adhering to some socially imposed norm of proper behaviour. We don't dance. We don't risk. We stay a million miles away from each other and away from the potential that we hold within ourselves, simply because we fear losing a conditional sense of safety.

We sacrifice our potential because we do not know that we are pure potential. If only we all knew this, then we could easily be fearless, bold, and persistent. We are permanent in only one way—the life potential that exists within us. This potential is unbreakable and unstoppable. It goes beyond our bodies and beyond our life spans. We cannot be defined by any temporary thing, nor destroyed by it. There is no need to avoid pain, because even pain cannot destroy our true identity.

We can, of course, have varying and cycling surface identities. We need these in order to live, to act, to relate. The temporary can be beautiful just like a flower is beautiful. When we try to find permanence in our external self, however, we face pain. We face pain because we cycle constantly between comfort and loss, certainty and confusion. What served you yesterday will not serve you today, but you hold on just because you need something to hold on to. Like this, our ignorance of ourselves keeps us from healing and happiness.

Within, you hold a tiny piece of eternity, a fraction of life, a mirror of the universe. You are pure potential. You do not have more potential than me, nor do I have more potential than you. Of course, time and space can interfere with our outward expression of that potential. I can be born without legs and you can be born into an era without pianos. Thus, I will never be a runner and you will never play. Our inner potential, however, does not change with outside circumstances. The permanent core is unchanged by the circumstances of the outer self. Within legless me is still the potential for a runner and within pianoless you is still the potential for a pianist. Potential is boundless. The expression of it is limited and temporary.

Knowing this, we can have compassion and appreciation for all the impermanent forms that drift in and out of our lives, our minds, our hearts. Knowing that this, too, shall pass is both sobering and comforting. Whether something is wonderful or horrible, the most harmful thought we can think is "Will this last forever?" It is harmful because, often, we seek for yes, when the answer is no. A well-known Rumi quote says: "Your task is not to seek for love, but merely to seek and find all the barriers within yourself that you have built against it." The ultimate barrier against love is the barrier of the constructed self. We try so hard to make ourselves lovable, and yet each layer of this mask puts another wall around us—a wall that keeps love out.

The tendency to preserve the external is very popular in our culture. Age-defying creams, lotions, and procedures empty wallets, all in a desperate attempt to preserve that which cannot be preserved. However misguided, these are responses to the inner call for permanence. There is nothing wrong with the call or with our urge to answer the call.

The problem lies in the way we answer it. To break out of our patterns of misery and delusion, we must be willing to look beyond the ready-made answers offered by those who seek to profit off our ignorance.

Changing your default self-understanding within this culture requires a drastic change of mindset, a complete revolution of thought. Perhaps the most helpful exercise in understanding the real meaning of permanence is going out into nature. The teachings of the nature path run directly counter to the teachings all around you. In our society, we deny death, we deny aging. We try to close our eyes to decay, degradation, and the end. We try to make good states last forever and bad states stay away forever. In nature, it is nothing like this. The dead branches lie comfortably among the live grass. The rocks sit among the frogs. The inanimate dirt plays easily with the hopping rabbits. All that is alive and all that is dead co-exist. There is no sweeping death or decay under the rug. Some things are living and others are dying. This, however, does not change the life energy within the forest. Things continue to grow because other things have died and these same things die because other things have lived. This is a comfortable and natural process. In nature, all that is temporary allows itself to be temporary without resistance. Behind each temporary form, such as an individual flower or a single bee, there is a steady, constant supply of life energy. This, and only this, is eternal. All else births and dies. At first glance, this may seem depressing. At first experience, it is the most beautiful thing.

*

Since the permanent self resides within, it does not need to be earned. It cannot be removed, created, or built. It is there, awaiting your acceptance just like a thirsty tree awaits your acceptance that it is a tree. Of course, it is not the acceptance itself that is being awaited; it is water for the tree and love for you. However, in order to know what to give, you must first know the nature of your recipient. Loving oneself is akin to nourishing oneself. Discovering the truth of who you are is the only way to love and care for yourself.

With a permanent self, all questions of deserving disappear. In our shame-filled society, we ask: do I deserve to be loved? Do I deserve to be accepted, cherished, or admired? When we look at ourselves through the permanent self, these questions seem silly. They seem as silly as asking—do I deserve to eat? Does a flower deserve sunshine? Does a bee deserve pollen? If I am, at the core, an essential part of the ever-present unity, how can I not deserve to be united? How can I not deserve to be something that I already am?

My external self, then, is my creation and my art project. It is my work and my play. It is my legacy and my show. It is my child that needs feeding and my house that needs decorating. It is not, however, my home. It is not my identity. It is not my true self. It is a necessity, yes, but it will never be stable. The child will leave the nest. The best paint job will crack. The best play will become boring. The best work will grow tedious. The best art will lose meaning. The greatest creation will decay. Behind all this, lies my true self.

Knowing this, I can do anything. This is the difference between a starving artist who is told to paint a very specific picture to get his next meal and a well-fed artist who paints because he is passionate about painting. This is what life becomes when we find our true home, when we open the gates of our minds and come into the feast of love within. There is no need to search for peace or happiness anywhere except for inside ourselves. With this, we gain the most sensational courage. We can do anything and be anyone. We can risk who we are right now for the possibility of experiencing something else tomorrow. We can sing out loud and speak our minds. We can do anything we truly desire, because there is no more need for fear.

Ironically, once you focus away from trying to find your individuality and put your attention towards your existing unity, your individuality will emerge. If I simply feed my roots thoughts of love, over time, I will find out what sort of tree I am to be here in this moment, in this body. This is a beautiful realization, but it is not my job. My job is just to water my roots and come out into the sun. All else flows effortlessly. It is not my job to criticize my external form or to deprive myself of nourishment. It is not my job to judge or punish. My job, my only job here in this moment, is to love myself and, by extension, to love others. My job is just to live and to realize that to live is to love. Even if I do not do my job, my essence will not change. If I fail to learn how to live, how to love, my external form will perish while my inner essence will live on in some other form. I cannot be broken. I cannot be killed. I cannot fail.

This is my identity. This is my core. I am infinite. I am permanent. I am unbreakable. There are other things that I'm told define me, but I am not attached to them. I may be told that I am attractive, but I do not make it part of my identity. I know that sexual attractiveness fades and I will not fade. I may be told that I am smart, but I do not make it part of my identity. I know that smart is just a word and that intelligence is not something fixed, but rather a process of learning from the world. Smart is not infinite. Growing is infinite. I may seek to learn and grow, but I will not make "smart" a part of my identity. I may be told that I'm stupid, ugly, worthless, fat, annoying, wrong, or bad. I do not make these a part of my identity either. They are not permanent, not infinite, and not true. They are simply judgments that others have made of me because that is how they judge themselves. I know that, as William Blake said, "If a thing loves, it is infinite." And that's me. I am infinite. I am loving. But, above all, I am always loved.

9

LOOKING AT YOU

If you can meet your relationship as you meet yourself, then you will see the flowering of the potential of what we call love relationships. Then, relationships are not, in fact, relationships. They are, in fact, oneself discovering oneself deeper, in different form, in different manifestation. Then, these so-called relationships are vehicles for the deepest truth.

GANGAJI

The same misunderstanding with which we search for ourselves, we search for relationships. The idea of perfection has been so deeply conditioned into our minds that anything else seems strange, unnatural, and even dangerous. The ideal self is something that gives us temporary comfort because it promises that, someday, we will be able to end all our suffering and find happiness. That day, of course, can be today, if we realize that we are already whole. While pursuing the ideal self, however, we have to wait. We have to buy something first. We have to apply some cream or get some sum of money before we can be happy. The idea of the soul mate is just like the idea of the ideal self. It gives us the comfort of hope, but it deprives us of the truth.

Most people these days show up for a first date with a mental checklist. Getting into a relationship is akin to passing a board exam—only the most qualified candidates make it through. The problem with searching for a soul mate this way is that we think we know what we want. We construct these lists of attributes that we desire from a perfect mate and we think, "If I just find that one, 'The One,' everything will be perfect." Then, when no one measures up or when those who seemed to measure up turn out to be just like everyone else, we blame ourselves for not choosing correctly or we blame our ex-partners for deceiving our intuition. The search for the soul mate, the perfect partner to complete you, is a bit like searching for the perfect food when you've got a giant ulcer in your stomach. No matter what you find, it will never be good enough.

The idea of two people completing one another is not entirely off base. Two people in a loving relationship can help one another heal, develop, and thrive. They can do so by providing an environment of safety, support, and unconditional acceptance. This does not, however, mean that they are halves meeting together as a whole. Such a concept leaves us all unhappy. Since we see others as we see ourselves, when we look at our own self as only half of some complete unit, how can anyone else be perfect? How can anyone be complete if I am incomplete, if we are all incomplete?

What we have done, essentially, is packaged one another. We have made one another into products, goals, destinations. This is no surprise since we live in a culture of commercialism. We have become the same as the products that we see on the shelves. The idea of the soul mate or the ideal partner is so attractive, the same way that the idea of the perfect car or the perfect house is attractive. It is a consequence of our itemization and objectification of each other. It is a direct by-product of our ignorance about our nature, about our inner purity, unity, and infinity.

Our hearts, like eager five year olds, plead for love and connection. Our minds are like ignorant parents. Fuelled by the advice of the other parents—the media, family, hearsay—the mind tells the heart that the best way to get love is to find the perfect lover. Collectively, this idea has spread because we've found no better way. This is how an addict's mind works. His heart wants joy, but the only way his mind has found to attain this joy is to buy it for $50. The mind does what it thinks will get the heart's desire, while the body slowly dies. And so we are addicts for what we call love. The inner child begs for connection and the conditioned mind says to have casual sex. The mind says to find the perfect person with the same interests and life goals. The mind preaches compatibility and pre-nuptial agreements. The heart keeps begging and the mind keeps trying, while the body slowly dies.

Fuelled by this delusion, our minds have turned our hearts into spoiled brats. The brat goes through toy after toy, believing that fun comes from getting the newest, shiniest thing. Like this, we go through partner after partner, becoming easily bored, dissatisfied, and craving something better. The spoiled child appears to get everything she wants, but she tantrums constantly. Call her ungrateful, but she just feels empty inside. She only begs for the newest, shiniest things because that is what she has been told will make her happy. She is unhappy because she wants her parents' time or to engage deeply in an interest. The child, however, does not know this. She cries and cries, while her parents buy and buy. Like this, we search for our soul mates. We crave the completion of the other because that's what we've been told we want. After all that, we are miserable because we don't really need the perfect person. We do not really need anyone to complete us. We just need to find out the truth about ourselves. We need to find out that we are not toys, not packages, not products. We all dream of being exactly what we are—powerful, beautiful, and worthy.

Our objectification of ourselves and each other has turned us simultaneously into the products on the shelves as well as the customers in the aisles. We are the spoiled brats crying for the new toy, we are the new toys, and we are the old toys going into the donation bin. At one point, we're in one place, the next we're in another. One moment we're satisfied, the next we're empty. One moment we're appreciated, the next we're ignored. All the while, we keep shopping around for someone who won't make us feel used. We browse for people like a child browses for toys. Who will make me the happiest? With whom will I maximally avoid boredom, satiation, and frustration? What do I know about how people who make me happy look like, act like, and sound like? What do I know about the ones who make me miserable? Are you that person? Will you make me happy or sad?

Since we are so busy thinking of each other as objects, we miss the truth of who we are. When we don't see each other as our true selves, we only purchase each other based on all the irrelevant details. Over time, we are bound to get buyer's remorse. Perhaps 3 months later or 3 years later, the customer will look at the product, the man will look at his wife, and wince. Suddenly, the package is nothing special. Suddenly, he finds it painful to look at her. There she is with all her faults and flaws, her pains and struggles. There she is and, now that I see that, I don't want her. I don't want her because she reminds me of myself, and I don't want to look at reminders of myself. The most passionate romances end when two people who have loved one another's projected illusions take off their masks. The masked man despises the flesh on the face of his partner only as much as he despises his own. The solution, the man thinks, is to find a better object.

Then, there are those who get discarded, again and again. The proposed solution for these people is to become higher quality objects. To avoid the feeling of having someone experience buyer's remorse over us, we are told to make ourselves better—to upgrade to a newer version. If only we can become skinnier, stronger, richer, funnier, or smarter, then we will be less likely to be replaced by a new, shiny toy. This, of course, fails, because the problem is not with the quality of the box we put around ourselves, but with the box itself.

One of the most important parts of sustaining a love relationship is to see the box for what it is. The box is there to train us to behave. To train a dog, we say, "Sit" and, when he does, we give him a treat. Without sitting, he gets no treat. He cannot get what he wants until he does what we want. These patterns, repeated, have the dog so well trained that he no longer requires a treat every single time. After a while, he just learns to obey. It becomes a habit.

Like this, love has become a treat. We all have an inner burning desire to connect with others. However, this desire is formless in our inner, ignorant child. The child simply feels the need. Then, the parent, the mind, comes along and gives the child a name for what she wants and gives her a blueprint for how to attain it. From the time that we're young, we begin to formulate an idea of what, exactly, we want and how, exactly, we can get it. Love becomes a destination, a goal, an entitlement. It is something we are told we can earn, if we are good at making ourselves lovable and at finding someone to love us. At the end of our journey of self-improvement and proper selection, we're told, is the prize: true love.

We see our goal in the distance. It is painted with silver and gold. Like Dorothy's friends, we set off to see the wizard, believing that we need to go far, far away to get what we want. All along the way, we're given directions as to how to best find love. Put on this mascara. Buy this ab stimulation belt. Buy this watch. Act sexy. Act disinterested. Wear this jacket. Sit. Lie down. You're so obedient. Maybe, one day, you'll get a treat.

Like dogs, we're trained with love. We're told to do all sorts of things that send abundant amounts of cash into someone's pockets. Our inner children crave connection. Since we are lacking in wise parental role models to tell the truth about love, unity, and humankind, we settle for the next best thing. We settle for the strangers around us who only want to manipulate us to get what they want. They do not care about whether or not we have love in our lives. They do not care about the giant gaping hole that we feel we have to stuff with food, money, sex, and mindless entertainment. They do not care about our inner children achieving their dreams. They do not care, not because they are bad people, but because we are just numbers on a sheet of paper and their job is to work with numbers on paper. In response to our dreams, they put us in dreamland. With our eyes closed and our bodies moving like machines, we keep reaching for love like a dog reaches for a biscuit or a horse reaches for a carrot. We are being very compliant, but we are not being truthful and we are not happy.

*

Author Jason Evert said it best: "Don't worry about finding your soul mate. Find yourself." "The One" is supposed to complete you. In reality, you need someone to complete you about as much as a car needs to be at a dealership or a piece of cake needs to be part of the cake. One person is a completely functioning unit. The inner potential within you is just like the inner potential within me. There is no completing you with me or myself with you. Two of the same cannot complete each other. There is nothing to complete. We are already complete, awaiting this recognition.

The idea of completing one another is an idea of dependence. You need me and I need you. In the dance of dependence, we do not bother to learn the steps because we spend all our time criticizing each other's inability to dance. This becomes tiresome. When we've had enough of that dynamic, in a rush of indignant fervour, "I need you" becomes "I don't need you, I don't need anyone." If I dance, I dance alone. Now, in the dance of independence, I stay away from people and people stay away from me. Here, I think I will find solace, but after some time, I become hopelessly dissatisfied. I feel lonely, but I think that the only way to be with others is to dance the tango of need and possessiveness. I stay alone or I plunge back into the madness. No matter what I do, it hurts. It hurts because neither complete dependence nor complete independence meets the needs of my soul. I know, inherently, that something else is possible, but I don't know what it is. I hunger for real love. I hunger to be self-sufficient and connected. I hunger for my essence. The essence of love is interdependence. We desperately crave to discover the truth—that we are already in perfect harmony with each other.

When we stop looking for someone to complete us, we find completion in ourselves. I am my soul and that is enough. I find power in my own truth, my own eyes. I feed my mind and my heart. I watch myself blossom into a beautiful organism which, externally, appears different from other organisms, just like there are different species of plants and animals. My external representation is completely unique to me, thus my struggles and my joys, my interests and my fears—they are all unique to me. When I allow myself to be completely open to the truth of who I am in infinity, my finite self blossoms beautifully and easily. I grow into my most beautiful external self when I open to unconditional, eternal love. I flourish when I realize I'm already complete.

When I do this, I am living an open life. I have an open mind, which allows me to have an open heart. Inside my head, my home is love. Effortlessly, I act out of love and I give out of love. I am a servant, bringer, and observer of love. I love myself and others with the same ease with which the earth revolves around the sun. When I look at people, I see their souls. I see them for who they really are and I treat them with respect, kindness, and compassion.

When I see someone who sees me back, there's a sort of meeting of minds and a resulting meeting of hearts. This is where we find the soul mate. My soul mate is someone who is at the same level of consciousness as I. His mind is open just like mine and his heart meets my heart. We live within the unity of love, both completely open to one another's permanent and impermanent truth. From here, we are like two voyagers who have come together on the path of love. We continue to be ourselves, to be complete within ourselves, and we begin to complement one another. We complement, we do not complete. We build our lives around supporting one another to heal and grow.

The key to loving relationships is to accept one another in permanence. The same way that we deeply crave a permanent identity, we crave a permanent relationship. We want the certainty of the bond. You want to know that, no matter what, your partner will be there for you. Within every lover, there's a question. That question is: "What if I...?" What if I lose my hair? What if I haven't any more money? What if I can't provide for you anymore? What if I lose my good looks? What if I gain fifty pounds? What if I can't make you laugh like I used to? What if I lose my job? What if I want to take more time to myself? What if I become disfigured? What if your parents told you to stop seeing me? What if you find someone better? What if you meet someone more attractive? What if this operation changes my body? What if aging changes my mind?

These questions haunt each and every member of every relationship, including the relationship with self. We drive ourselves crazy with conditional acceptance, conditional "love" (which is really not love at all). We say, "I will only love you if..." and this breeds misery in our relationships with ourselves as well as with others. Looking at myself in the mirror is the same as looking at you. If I want to be happy, then the answer to "What if I...?" must be "I will still love you." No matter what the question is, I will still love you. No matter what happens to you and no matter what you do, I will still love you. I will look at you as I look at you now, no matter how much you change. That is because I see who you really are. You are who I am. You are eternal, beautiful, and real. You can never lose my love.

Mary Haskell summarized this kind of relationship beautifully: "Nothing you become will disappoint me; I have no preconception that I'd like to see you be or do. I have no desire to foresee you, only to discover you. You can't disappoint me."

This, at the core, is what we all want from ourselves and what we all so desperately crave from one another. The idea of the soul mate, though it seems to suggest a lifetime of love, detracts us away from this. We throw away real people searching for the "perfect" person the same way that we throw ourselves away searching for our "perfect" self. In love, for self and for other, there can only be unconditional acceptance. Every "What if I...?" must be met with love, always love. To come together like this, to see each other like this, is the only way to have a satisfying relationship.

It is not until you learn to look at yourself through the truth of who you are that you can look at someone else. When you discover your own self, you will see that same infinite potential in your lover's eyes. While what we usually do is project onto others, this is not projection. To project is to drown out what is there with what we put in its place. The love mindset eases not projection, but recognition. We do not merely conceal one false identity with another. Looking with eyes of love is about not only looking, but seeing. It is about seeing the person in front of you by recognizing them as an equal. A soul mate is not found. A soul mate is recognized.

10

SELF-PROTECTIVE SELF-DESTRUCTION

Perhaps all the dragons in our lives are princesses who are only waiting to see us act, just once, with beauty and courage. Perhaps everything that frightens us is, in its deepest essence, something helpless that wants our love.

RAINER MARIA RILKE

It is not only the illusion of perfection that keeps us lonely. It is also the illusion of injury. I do not want to get closer to you because you can hurt me. In fact, every other "You" has hurt me, so why wouldn't you? I see, in you, my father, my ex, my rapist, my captor, my foe. I see in you my anger, my imperfection, my lies. I see, in you, myself and every person I've ever known. This scares me away from you. This convinces me that you will hurt me and so I back away. I keep a certain distance, so that you never, ever have to see me for who I am. If you did, you might reject me or, even worse, I may grow dependent on you. I may grow such a bond with you that it will not be simple to break. Best to stay distant. Best to stay safe.

These sorts of thoughts are our primary line of defence against the pain that we associate with relationships. Our mind is much like our immune system. An organism that receives a dose of poison immediately begins to fight. The immune system sends out an army of cells to kill the intruding venom, cleanses the body of the poison's toxic effects, and produces antibodies to protect us against it in the future. The first attack is always the harshest. If an organism survives, it is more prepared the second time around. Now, there are antibodies that act like trained soldiers. No longer is the attacker coming into an open gateway. Now, there are troops, tanks, and bayonets. The body is designed in such a way that our muscles, tissues, and organs stay maximally protected. In order to do this, the immune system detects potential dangers and carefully executes plans to keep us safe.

The immune system has antibodies and the mind has fear. When we encounter a painful situation for the first time, we are vulnerable, open, and unprepared. We are completely receptive and we receive the full dose of hurt that comes from the situation. Think back to your first experience of public humiliation. Look at your first love. Remember the first time that you were ever rejected, hit, or excluded. If you are like most people, you remember those experiences vividly. There is much truth to the common saying that the first cut is the deepest. Our first loves were usually the most painful because, back then, we didn't guard ourselves. We left our hearts completely open and, at some point, we were struck deeply and painfully. We tend to react to any kind of pain by protecting ourselves. After all, we are adaptive organisms. We avoid pain and seek pleasure.

The mind hears the heart's cry. Like a knight to the rescue, the mind charges in to kill the monstrous beasts that ail the aching heart and to prevent them from coming in the future. Seeking only to serve the heart's interests, the mind performs its logical calculations in response to the heart's request. Like the immune system does a scan and determines the composition of the poison before it creates antibodies, the mind scans the situation that produced pain to determine the source. The mind is a master detective. It searches for what happened immediately before the pain. It seeks for unusual or unique conditions that would have caused pain in that situation and not in others. It looks back at memories and tries to find other factors that have contributed to painful feelings, trying always to find patterns, cycles, causes and effects. Soon enough, the mind finds an answer. Signed and sealed, it passes its deduction over to the heart. The mind's conclusion reads like a simple statement of equivalence. It says, for example, that intimacy equals pain. The heart does not want to feel pain and the mind, as a loving parent, wants to help the heart achieve its desire. Thus, the mind makes a plan. To avoid pain, we will have to avoid intimacy. Then, the mind takes on the task of searching, in every moment, for signs of impending intimacy. When it locates any such evidence, a self-protective thought occurs, such as "I can get really hurt here." This triggers the emotion of fear, which automatically triggers withdrawal. The mind protects us from pain by triggering fear where it senses danger.

Fear is an antibody. It is a line of defence. Fear, in essence, is not good or bad. It has earned a bad reputation because of its tendency to interfere with our functioning, but truly, fear is useful. Fear is what keeps you from putting your hand onto a hot stove or jumping headfirst into traffic. Fear is useful just like antibodies are useful. However, even antibodies—which are usually helpful—can become deadly. Sometimes, antibodies do not stop growing when the poison or virus is gone. Sometimes they do not even form in response to a real virus, but to the illusion of a perceived virus. Thus, the antibodies keep replicating and begin attacking the body. This is called an autoimmune disease. These sorts of diseases, where the body attacks itself, originate in the very same system that protects the body. That which is supposed to keep us safe can become the most dangerous thing.

This is the role that fear has come to play in most relationships. The first time, we were vulnerable. The second time, we learned our lesson. We quickly learned to associate pain with men, relationships, sex, women, vulnerability, love. Then, we set to protecting ourselves from pain with surges of fear in the face of these perceived dangers. We stay away from each other believing that isolation is safety. We keep our hearts protected believing that, if we let our loving emotions free, we will be taken advantage of, hurt, or rejected. Over time, the same fear that used to protect us has now spread into every part of our experience. Fear becomes a self-destructive defence mechanism.

*

Many spiritual teachers have named fear, rather than hate, as the opposite of love. Though I would say that love has no opposite, such a comparison has merit. Love is the ultimate unity. It is the ever-present connection. Fear is the ultimate division. It is the parent of disconnection. Love brings us close and fear drives us apart. Love makes us approach and fear makes us move away. Thinking of love, we remember eternity, permanence, and stability. Thinking of fear, we remember death, rupture, and uncertainty. Feeling love, we want to be together. Feeling fear, we want to be alone. Focusing on love makes us peaceful and generous. Focusing on fear makes us paranoid and violent.

Fear is part of a survival system that seeks to preserve our impermanent form. Fear aids the continuation of an organism's livelihood. Though it cannot keep us alive for too long—for we all must die—fear certainly seeks to prolong the process. While love awareness acknowledges the permanent self, fear awareness acknowledges only the impermanent self. Fear is living externally, while love is living internally. For people that try to live their lives simply from an external identity, fear drives their reality. Over and over, they face the possibility of losing their external form. They react by protecting themselves more securely, always seeking the newest hiding spots, the best weapons, and the strongest shields.

Fear quickly becomes a mindset. Within this mindset, awareness turns completely towards a distorted reality. In this reality, nothing exists outside of possible dangers, and the dangers themselves are grossly distorted and overemphasized. Threatening situations are anticipated days and miles before they come. What used to be a trigger or two becomes an entire interlocked universe of people, places, phrases, and memories that send waves of fear all over the body. The fear-minded individual is always in a state of panic, always with one hand on the trigger, always ready to run. There is no room for connection or joy. There is no room for reality. Life, for the fear-minded, is a game of instinct and survival.

Fear keeps us from our potential. Our brains allow us to experience deep consciousness and loving awareness. We are not meant to live like rats, always erring on the side of caution and scurrying away from passers-by. If the permanent part of us, before acquiring its impermanent form, could have any consciousness over the structure it was receiving, it would be enthralled to receive the human form. Of all the impermanence on the earth, the human body holds within it the greatest capacity for experiencing life to the fullest.

Fear is not only a waste of our valuable potential; it also ironically tends to put us into more danger than living fearlessly. The fear mindset is like living in an armoured fortress on top of a hill surrounded by fifty armies, always ready to attack. In the tense silence of awaiting the attacker, sometimes a soldier accidentally hits the trigger and, suddenly, there is a shootout. This is the autoimmune disease. This is the illness of fear. In the absence of some outside danger or villain, the self becomes a threat.

Fear-driven people become self-destructive. Fuelled by the hunger of love deprivation and constantly vigilant, they live as if disaster is always imminent. Fear, then, becomes a self-fulfilling prophecy. Thinking that there is something to be avoided manifests something to avoid. Even if the danger we are running from is completely imagined, our fear response is still rewarded. We may think that we're doing something useful and productive, but really we're just running away from ghosts, mirages, illusions. The relationships we have in the fear mindset are not with real people. We project our fears onto the person we're with. Then, our projections push them into the very role that we dread. To expect the worst from someone is the worst insult. It is worse than making a slur to their character. A negative expectation says—not only is this how I see you, but this is how you'll always be. Often, the fearful and the mistrustful push their partners miles away with accusations. Then, when the pushes are successful, the fear mindset strengthens. Those who live in fear create their own enemies.

It is impossible to love someone and to fear her. These are not compatible states. We may think that we love someone that we fear or fear someone that we love, but this is not love. We do not really see him. If we see someone for who he is, we accept him as part of ourselves. Perhaps we do not choose to be around him, but this comes from a conscious choice, not an automatic fear response. If you see your own self for who you are and see others for who they are, there is nothing to fear. To love yourself and others is to be fearless. Love awareness makes it very clear that nothing and no one can ever hurt you. The real you cannot be harmed.

This is not to say that we should not jump out of the way of harm or avoid dangerous situations. The fetus does not seek to come out of the womb before her time is up. Likewise, we should not seek to meet our grave before it is time either. The key is to spend the time we have experiencing that which this world has to offer. The offer of life is not to extend it for as long of a time as possible at any cost, but to enjoy its fruits and spread their seeds in the short time that we are here. To live a long life of fear is nothing to a short life of love. Living in fear is like going to a party and spending the whole thing in the stall of the bathroom. The fear mindset is making love while worrying about what the other will think instead of using that moment to connect and enjoy. Fear is letting go of your dreams and ambitions simply because you do not realize that the pain of failure can't destroy you. All in all, fear is a waste of time. To live with the disease of fear is a waste of a life.

*

Like love, most people think of fear as an emotion. Fearful emotions, however, are only one part of the experience of fear. Any experience, whether it is fear, love, or anger, contains three components: thoughts, emotions, and actions. You get a loving thought, which triggers the feeling of love, which drives you to be kind. You get an angry thought, which triggers the emotion of anger, which makes you throw things. Fear, like all other experiences, follows this three-step sequence: thought to emotion to action. You get a fearful thought, which triggers the emotional response, which then makes you withdraw. You think, "I can get hurt," your heart hammers, and you run away. You think, "This isn't safe," your pulse speeds, and you excuse yourself.

The way that most people treat fear-related illnesses, such as anxiety or panic disorder, is by taking medications. Medications only interfere between the first and second step. They come between the thought and the emotion, thereby loosening the link between the two. A hypochondriac thinks "I'm dying!" and gets a panic attack. A hypochondriac on anxiety medications thinks, "I'm dying!" and feels nothing. This sort of treatment for fear-related mind infestations is so common that we hardly question it. After all, it seems to help. Right?

The problem with using this approach exclusively is that the fear-driven thought blocks the love-driven thought. All mindsets begin with thoughts. Although the fear mindset cannot develop if the thoughts do not trigger emotions, the love mindset cannot develop either since there are no loving thoughts. A fear-driven thought comes and the roots still receive poison. Even if some special procedure prevents the poison from being absorbed into the roots, this procedure does not provide water. The absence of pain does not automatically imply the presence of pleasure. The absence of the fear reaction does not manifest love awareness. It just numbs the emotion. In today's world, it is tempting to follow suit and artificially numb the emotions you don't want while inducing the ones that you do want. The problem is that pushing pleasure into your veins will not get you out of quicksand, nor will blocking pain bring you relief. The solutions do not lie in the world of emotions, but rather in the world of thoughts.

If you found yourself watering a tree with poison, the first thing to do would be to stop using the poison. The second thing would be to start using water. This process is simple but, once again, not necessarily easy. In the mind, unlike the tree, the poison will return. You will know this if you've ever tried to augment your thoughts. The ones that you try to release still keep coming.

Here is where the importance of love and permanent identity come into play. When we're struggling, we become homesick. To recover from the illness of fear, just like any illness, we're much more likely to become healthy within the safety and comfort of our home. When you hear fearful thoughts, remember that it is simply your inner cry for permanence directing into your external self. Fear is just a misunderstanding of your immortality. When you feel fear, take a moment to remember that, in the end, there is absolutely nothing to fear. Remember who you really are. You cannot be destroyed or hurt. You cannot be harmed or killed. You, the real you, will always be present and powerful. In this place, in this warm cavern that the lone-minded call home, we can watch the fearful thought roll by as if it's a gust of wind outside of our well-sealed windows. The thought comes, but it does not strike deep into our feelings to drive compulsive actions. It lives outside of our safe, protected, permanent home. By remembering yourself, you open yourself to the healing energy of love and you give yourself resilience against the disease of fear.

What happens when you return to your core is that your external self relaxes. In order to act on fear (or any other emotion), your muscles must be active. Complete relaxation inhibits action. This is exactly the place in which you find yourself when you embrace your authentic self in a time of fear. Your inner self is like a raised rock in the middle of a stampede. You climb onto the rock and watch the stampede go by. You are perfectly safe, despite all the danger around you. You are calm and relaxed, even though moving even a few inches in any direction would mean a certain death. In such a space, there is no way for fear to sweep you up and make you either attack or run. If fearful thoughts are a fishhook that seeks to grasp you and drag you along, love is the ultimate resilience. With the love mindset, you cannot be hooked like a fish, because you are not the fish. You are the water. The hook moves freely through you and grasps nothing. It cannot catch you, kill you, or hurt you. You cannot be caught, killed, or hurt.

When we perceive ourselves as essential parts of an ever-present unity, there is nothing to lose. There is nothing to fear. To fear, inside the love mindset, is to lose precious moments of life within the external form. Of course, this does not mean that, by thinking loving thoughts, you will never feel fear again. Of course, you will still feel it, each time that you accidentally believe your fearful thoughts. But with your compass set on love, you will soon remember yourself, and your experience of falling into fear will serve to solidify your understanding of those thoughts as toxic.

To face fear from your core requires you to be vulnerable. This means you will experience pain. But what is pain? It is simply a feeling. It is not forever. If you get pain from some person or thing too many times, you can always walk away. To risk a lifetime without pleasure simply to avoid pain is ludicrous. To sacrifice that which is true, eternal, and ever-present in order to avoid something temporary and fleeting is self-destructive. To waste a life with fear is, really, the scariest thing.

11

BANDAGE WORSHIP

Eventually you will come to understand that love heals everything, and love is all there is.

GARY ZUKAV

Of all the relationships in my life, my most intimate and long-standing one was my relationship with my wounds. It was not a happy relationship, nor a loving one, but it was a relationship nonetheless. My wounds and I, we spent over a decade together. Even the most obnoxious sidekick becomes comforting after that many years of just showing up at your side. If you wake up every day with the same old biting pain and the same old tired story of who you are, it all becomes part of the scenery. Just the way things are.

As a child, when I got hurt, I'd hold out my bruised knuckle to my mother's lips. Somewhere inside that childish ritual lies a hint of awareness about our inner nature. We know that love heals all wounds. As a kid, I was just doing what I had seen the adults do. When you get hurt, you ask for love. That worked for me, at least for a while.

As children, we open our hearts unconditionally. We take whatever we are given. We trust that what we are being given is good for us. After a while, however, I was no longer getting little scratches. I was getting deep, raw cuts. Opening myself led me into whirlwinds of pain. I didn't know what to do. I held my wounds out to my mother, but all I got was anger and rejection. Confused, I held my wounds out to others only to be met with the same sorts of reactions—laughter, anger, indifference. What used to help was no longer effective. The wounds became more and more serious as I grew older. Just to take away the blinding pain of walking around with open injuries exposed to the world, I put bandages on them. At the time, this seemed like a great idea. The pain was gone and the wounds were covered. I breathed a sigh of relief.

A little while later, the pain came back. From underneath the bandages, I felt the throbbing pulse of infection. Confused and frightened, I put on another bandage, and then another. Each application would help for a while, but soon enough, the same old pain would return. Though the bandages would conceal the cut, the skin underneath was red and infected. Sometimes, I would look at my bandages and see the swollen skin around them. I would get frightened. The mere sight of my injuries gave me anxiety. Having no other options in sight, I just put on more bandages. Not knowing how to heal, I settled for removing the discomfort of fear and pain.

Most people thought I was strange. After all, who wants to be around a girl covered in bandages? For a while, I thought: no one. Then, I found other bandaged people, people just like me. When I found them, I rejoiced. Finally, some company! Finally, people who would understand me, talk to me, and relate to me! There, within the confines of dark walls and equally dark stories, I found solace in similarity. There, too, I learned a thing or two about being wounded, about being bandaged.

The first thing I learned was that every set of bandages needed a story. I came up with my own set of excuses and justifications. I gathered the most shocking and horrific moments of my life and conveniently packaged them into a narrative. As time went on, I altered the story. Some bits were just too raw, too real for even the wounded. I took those parts out. Other parts, however, never ceased to shock and impress. Those, I exaggerated. In the world of wounds and stories, I also learned about bandages. I learned all the newest tips and tricks—how to cover my wounds with style and mystery, how to hide in plain sight, how to live through a mask. I learned to be dark and to love being dark. Soon enough, I was covered in bandages head-to-toe. I could have been anyone, even a plastic doll. There was nothing human about me, except that deep down under all those layers, I still needed love.

In a community of bandage worshippers, neglect of the external self is normal. Everyone stuffs themselves full of whatever they can get their hands on, anything that helps them avoid themselves. Everyone lies, hides, and hates themselves. Everyone has their own, personally branded, way of self-destructing. They define themselves by their wounds. In that place, when we saw someone who wasn't covered in bandages, someone we called "normal," we'd assume them to be boring, stupid, or deficient somehow. We had to. We had to believe that what we were doing was right. We had to do anything that we could to keep putting on those bandages, to keep hiding from the pain.

Relationships there were horribly painful. We would try to come together, but the sores under the bandages hurt too much. We were stuck and helpless. If we stayed distant, we felt empty. If we came together, we writhed in pain. Again and again, we tried to love each other, but we could not figure out how—at least that was the excuse. I'm not sure if this is true, but I suspect now that we all knew, deep down, what we needed to do. We just didn't want to admit it. We just kept bandaging and hurting, lying and hiding.

After a while, bandages just weren't enough. I had learned all the best ways to use them, but the skin underneath was now covered in pus and blood-filled blisters that would pop on contact. Just walking around, people would bump into me and rub my wounds through the bandages. I'd exclaim in shock and pain. It became harder and harder to keep a straight face everywhere I went. These incidents became more and more frequent as the wounds spread under the cover-up.

That was when I met *her*. In a crowd covered with mere gauze, she was gleaming with steel. Her face never showed pain. When people brushed by her, they winced. She didn't. She would look down at them and laugh. At that moment, I suddenly noticed that, no matter how thick their bandages were, all the people in my little world were walking around with pain in their eyes—except for her. She didn't have pain. Her eyes were cold and empty. From the moment I first saw her, I knew that I wanted to be just like her.

Soon enough, I became a perfect replica. I had my very own suit of armour. I became the queen of the bandage worshippers. They looked up to me because I had what they wanted—freedom from pain. Some of them left, and the rest had to get armour of their own. After all, a girl who can't feel emotions is just not safe to be around for people who can. They had to either get their own protection or get away from me.

Inside the armour, I was numb. I couldn't feel the outside world and I couldn't feel my skin. There was no more pain, but there was no more pleasure either. I was numb and empty. I knew that, no matter how much I tried to hide it, underneath all that armour, I was dying. My real flesh was oozing toxic sludge. My body was decaying and I didn't have much time. To the bandage worshippers, I looked like I had everything under control. I knew—and all the healthy people who saw me knew—that it was all an armoured charade.

I tried to ignore the truth, but no one can do that for very long. I lived in my metal armour for as long as I could, before I got too weak to move, too weak to lie, too weak to play the game anymore. In every sickness, there comes a point of no return. Every bandaged, wounded person whose skin is on the point of necrosis has to make a choice: let it kill me or let me heal, change or die. At that moment, the risk of vulnerability suddenly became secondary to the risk of remaining hidden. There, I disassembled the armour. There, I peeled off the bandages, one by one, crying and screaming. Each one would take with it chunks of my flesh. Parts of me were already dead and many others were close.

Those were some of the most painful moments of my life and, now, I still find little pieces of bandages lodged in my skin or hidden in my old possessions. The bandages did not disappear simply because I had an awakening, and neither did the pain. What changed was my perception. Instead of numbing and hiding, I took the pain of raw, exposed wounds for what it was: necessary. It was the only way to heal. The only way to heal any wound is to keep it open, exposed. Temporary, but excruciating, pain is the price of healing. The bandages may cover it up for just a moment, but in the end, they only become a sick addiction.

My story is not unique. Most of the people who are passionate about healing others, about helping others find love, truth, and happiness have known love hunger. A healer is someone who seeks to be the light that she wishes she had in her darkest moments. When you're starving to death and you suddenly find food, it's a miracle. That's what this was. It was a miracle. I don't know if you've ever experienced one of those, but when you do, you just want to share it with the world.

*

I learned, down the road, that my little community of bandage worshippers was actually quite radical. Some of the things that went on there were grotesque and unfamiliar to the average person. Nonetheless, bandage worship and armouring are common in all corners of our society. We live in a world of victims and judges. The tough façade and the "poor me" story have spread into our personalities as if we've all been cast in a giant play. We are all so hurt, so damaged, but we don't know how to get out. We don't know how to heal in the long-term, so we just learn to numb our pain in the short-term. If there was an award for most creative temporary "fixes" for emotional pain, I bet you, like me, would have a ready list of nominees. If you're anything like me, as well, you'd put yourself—past or present—somewhere near the top.

Our tendency to settle for numbing our emotional pain is not self-sabotage. Sabotage implies intent. It is more like blind self-destruction. We don't have a better way, so we do what we can. Our minds tell our eyes what to see and our hands what to do. When your mind thinks that the only way out is to run—that's exactly what you'll do. You will do whatever your mind thinks is best. In a culture full of people who are so deeply hurt and frightened to the bone, avoiding healing is normal. Healing isn't something most people do these days. Medicate, yes. Delay, yes. Complain, yes. Heal? Rarely.

Though we know, instinctively, that our emotional wounds, like our physical wounds, need to be exposed to heal, there is a strong fear of the act. This is the fear of hurt. If I expose my wound, painful and infected, I will feel more pain. So I hide it. Perhaps I am aware that hiding it makes it worse in the long run, but I get these images, feelings, and ideas about what will happen if I expose myself. Since these are just in my imagination, they trump anything that happens in real life. The scariest horror movies are the ones where the brutality is left up to our imagination. When we see something horrible in reality, it is rarely as horrible as our memory of it. The mind can warp anything, and the resulting distortion can give us feelings of fear so powerful that they completely override what is truly there. The warped ideas in our heads are like imaginary monsters in the dark. When we run away from them, we can imagine that we've escaped horrible beasts, when we've only darted away from shadows. Each time we run away from an illusion, our distorted ideas strengthen. In fear, we feel like we are running away from some worthy opponent, when really we are running from salvation.

Of course, our fear is not without cause. Bandaging wounds by keeping them out of sight and armouring ourselves to keep from the pain are not just rituals of the outcasts. These are common practices in our society, as common as women wearing makeup and men wearing pants. Of course, in other cultures, women do not wear makeup and men do not wear pants. However, everywhere we look, there's a certain norm. Whether or not we're conscious of it, fitting into the norm gives us comfort. Having no idea how to get comfort within our own minds, we settle for the comfort of conformity. We think that if we can just be the same as everyone else, if we can just fit in, then maybe we can be loved and accepted. This thought process goes on below the surface, out of ordinary conscious awareness. Our minds simply do a survey of our surroundings and seek for the best way to unite. If we cannot fit ourselves into the larger norm, we'll shape ourselves to fit into some alternative norm. In any case, when we conform, we do not relate based on our personal truth and we do not relate in love.

We are not built to hide. Look at how open a young child is about his tears, fears, and hurts. He is shameless and fearless about seeking healing and connection. Concealing ourselves is a behaviour that is heavily conditioned. It is not natural. It has taken thousands of thoughts over the course of a lifetime to hammer into our heads that we are not safe, we are not good enough, and we are doomed to suffer. At first, we do not believe the cynical teachings we hear from the authorities. Then, we have an experience that hurts us. We think, "Well, maybe it *is* true. Maybe I really can't trust people." Years later, we find ourselves bandaged and armoured just like everyone else. Then, we spread our negative, cold message to our friends, our families, our children. We precipitate the lie because we believe it. In these cycles, we are stuck, sick, and miserable. The same thoughts that we use to keep ourselves hidden, we then utter to others. We water our own roots with poison and, since poison is all we have, we water others' roots with poison too. We have kept on like this for so long that, for some people, water is becoming an urban legend.

It is almost as if we are all playing a game of hide-and-go-seek. We all hide, expecting to be found, but no one has been labelled the seeker. We stand behind the wall, at first excited, then worried, then bored, then anxious, then angry. We hide and hide. After a while, the game is not fun anymore. Where is my seeker? Where is the person who is supposed to come find me here in my protected shell and cut me open? Where is that one who will make me trust again, make me comfortable, make me feel whole? Some people rot on the spot, waiting for the seeker that never comes. The most important truth that I can relate to you, if you are hiding and waiting, is that the seeker is *you* and the world, behind so many walls, awaits.

*

The authentic self does not need to heal. People speak of healing their inner child, but this does not refer to the soul. It refers to emotions, especially emotions hidden under layers of bandages and armour. The soul does not need healing just like love does not need to be replenished. The soul, like love, must be turned towards. It only needs to be remembered, realized, and lived through. There is no need to reconstruct it, only to attend to it.

Much of our healing avoidance goes on because we try to connect in the wrong way. We know, intuitively, that what we need to do is unite, so our minds go searching for similarities. There, we tend to find conformity. The mind finds that everyone else seems to be doing fine and we, with our wounds, are strange and should remain silent. Even if our intuition leads us to open ourselves to someone, the emotional pain that results from rejection reinforces the mind's belief that we need to hide. Then, when someone else comes and opens up to us, we reject her automatically. We can never treat another better than we treat ourselves. As long as we deny healing to our own self, we will deny it to the world. Like this, we cycle round and round. We continue to seek for connection in conformity. We conform to shame and distance, isolation and depravity, gluttony and misery. We are all working together to perpetuate a reality that none of us enjoy or benefit from.

The key to healing is not to rid ourselves of the instinct to conform. We conform because we seek to connect. We know that we must unite to heal just like a child knows that love heals all. We only need to look for unity where it actually lies. Two life forms can appear to be drastically different while being unified parts of the same process, the same larger picture. There is a unity between tree and river, tiger and dandelion, branch and wind. They look nothing alike and behave nothing alike, but they are more similar than different. They unite in life, in love.

When we look at ourselves and others like this, we can see beyond the bandages and armour. We see through to the permanent core. This vision, this mindset, gives us instant compassion. When you have a safe, impenetrable core to hold on to, all you must do is wait. All paint takes time to dry and all wounds take time to heal. We are willing to take this time if we feel safe. More than anything, we are afraid to open up to our own reflections and to open up to other people, because we equate vulnerability with a possible death. It could hurt me so much that I'll never recover, we think. It could be so painful, so much more painful than the pain of rotting from the inside. It is common to choose to stay "safe" because opening up is "dangerous."

If, however, you can re-orient your mind's ideas of life and death, of safety and danger, it is a different story. Such a complete revolution of ideas has the power to change your life. Anaïs Nin spoke of such a transformation. "And the day came," she said, "when the risk to remain tight in a bud was more painful than the risk it took to blossom." Some say that a person must hit rock bottom before she can change. While I do not agree that this is a pre-requisite to healing for everyone—perhaps only for persons as stubborn as my former self—there is a reason that rock bottom often leads to change. For most people, it is not until they have to decide be-tween life and death that they consider redefining what it means to "live" and what it means to "die." Those who have spent a lifetime dying in the name of staying alive suddenly understand that what used to seem dangerous is actually the safest haven, and vice versa.

The answer to healing your pain is to open up—first to your reflection, then to others. Along this journey, the same old fearful thoughts will return. If you accept them as true, they will set you back. If, however, you allow yourself to experience those thoughts and feelings while holding on to a deeper truth, you will feel your wholeness more powerfully than ever. When you allow yourself to feel pain, you find what is beyond that pain.

In the end, no matter how excruciating it is, pain is temporary. No matter how much you cry, the tears will dry. No matter how many nightmares, flashbacks, visions, or terrors you endure, they will pass. To weather these in order to gain the peace you deserve—this is not a risk. To waste the time you have in this body, never showing your truth to yourself or anyone else, living in fearful misery— this is really the most dangerous thing you can do. Bandages and armour seem to provide safety in the form of temporary relief. However, the persistence of the temporary always depends on the perma- nent. Without a conscious and wilful turning towards that which is permanent, the temporary will not be relieved, fixed, or extended for long. The trees depend on the sun. The fish depend on water. You, me, and all other people—we depend on love. To find the joy and healing you seek, turn towards your origin and nourishment, your birthright and legacy, your one and only truth.

12.

THE VILLAIN

Those who are hardest to love need it the most.

SOCRATES

The steadiest supply of fearful poison comes out of our media in the form of "facts" called the news. Those who watch the news religiously also tend to believe that the world is a horrible place dominated by equally horrible people. When I suggest to them that the world is a beautiful place, I'm often met by condescending eyes and headshakes. They say to me, with furrowed brows and crossed arms, "Obviously, you do not know what is *really* happening here." More than a few times after my transformation, I have been called naïve, childish, and silly.

"Don't you know," they say, "that there are bad people out there who do bad things? You never know where these bad people might emerge. They might come out of a prison, an open window, or out of your own womb. The danger could befall any of us, so we must err on the side of caution."

All in all, it seems that most people have simply failed to grow out of believing in villains. Almost a year ago, I heard about a young boy who had shot up a school, killing twenty young children. I set my mind on cultivating compassion for the children, their families, and the boy. I thought of how isolated, angry, and troubled he must have been in order to resort to such measures. Before my breakdown, I would never have thought this way or even tried to think this way. I would have just blamed and raged, which is exactly what I watched everyone around me do. Over the course of that day, I came face-to-face with judgement, rage, and resentment unlike anything I'd ever seen. In response to the violence, people felt violent. Some described, in gruelling details, how they would have harmed the killer if he had not taken his own life. Others simply settled for tirades of adjectives. Even more disturbing than the violent responses were the submissive ones. One well-known news source claimed that people were overreacting because, the truth of the matter was, shootings will always happen. We cannot predict them. We cannot stop them. We may as well get used to them. It seems that, when it comes to violence, we are also stuck in violent resistance and passive submission. All the while, the real culprit goes unnoticed.

The hypothesized solutions to violence include gun regulations and more mental health resources, but these are only Band-Aids. They treat the symptoms and not the cause. In the world of so-called villains, what we need is not another hero. What we need is to stop the influx of people who dress themselves as menaces and proceed to harm others. To do so would require us to see those who hurt people as violently resisting their love deprivation. Instead of fighting and resisting them as if they are purposefully attacking us, we can see them as hungry. This, in essence, is the meaning of compassion. Compassion is a response that comes from love awareness, which allows us to see all the suffering in the world as the result of love hunger. When we see this, we not only forgive those who have hurt us, but we also have a desire to help them heal. In the love mindset, there are no villains. Villains can only live within the misunderstood, polluted mind.

*

Living in a world of villains, one believes in selective love. This is when I love you, but I hate him. I love you, but I hate my mother. I love you, but I hate the murderer on the television. I love you, but I hate myself. I love you, but I hate all the other people on this miserable planet. After a while, I don't love *you* anymore. I wonder why. In the apt words of writer Jerry Spinelli: "If you learn to hate one or two persons… you'll soon hate millions of people."

Thoughts of the human being, whether it is self or other, inevitably end up representing your mindset about both yourself and the other. There is no escape from this formula. The relationship with any human is the relationship with all humans. If I believe in villains, then I, too, am a villain. If I believe in bad-natured, evil people, then I fear that bad nature and evil inside myself. If I think that some people don't deserve to be loved or appreciated, then I see myself as a person who does not deserve to be loved or appreciated. This understanding may not be conscious. We tend to run from these parts of ourselves. The mind, with its brilliant workings, figures out the most effective way to avoid our own negative self-image. Its genius plan is to pick out the traits we hate about ourselves in the people around us. This gives us a break from looking at our own reflection. Thus, we live in a culture of judgment, gossip, hatred, and apathy. It is not that we are purposefully cruel to each other. We are, first, cruel to ourselves.

The villain within is often so concealed that all a person can see are the villains around him. He externalizes his pain into three kinds of villains. The first is the distant villain on the mountaintop. This is the murderer on the news, the long-dead serial killer who lived in his town, the tyrannical leader of some faraway country. The distant villain is the one he's never met and isn't likely to meet. The second is the remembered villain. This is the estranged parent, the abusive ex, the attacker, the rapist, the ex-friend. He may run into the remembered villain occasionally in real life, but most of the drama happens in his memories. Finally, the third kind is the real-life villain. This is someone he faces every day.

This is his boss, his father, his wife. The real-life villain may even be a hallucination.

Anyone with villains tends to have more than just one and more than one in each category. Every day is painful for someone who believes in evil people. She is so busy hating and hating. Her life is full of anger, indignation, and frustration. Her villain thoughts multiply as her collection of distant, remembered, and real-life villains grows like a tumour. Someone bumps into her on the street, or a grocery store clerk gives her back the wrong change and, suddenly, there's a new villain. She turns on the television, opens a magazine, gets stuck in a traffic jam, visits family, and does all sorts of regular, everyday things, in each one finding new villains and triggers for memories of old ones. These patterns only intensify over time. They do not dissipate. She waters her roots with hateful thoughts, thus she grows hateful. She can grow into nothing except the product of that which she feeds herself.

Villain thoughts are a kind of addiction. They are the by-product of self-loathing so powerful that it has externalized. It is the same thought with a different pronoun. The hateful person says

"You," but he means "I." The bullied become the bullies. For victims, we all tend to have compassion, but for bullies most people have a hard heart. Bullies, however, always go through the victim stage. No one proceeds to hate others without, first, hating himself. Then, when he begins to hate others, others hate him back. This gives him more to hate about them and about himself. This goes on and on.

Hateful thoughts don't just spread like a disease within one mind; they spread through families, workplaces, and entire societies. Pronouns are a technicality. When we hear some label or judgment, we immediately try it on. If it fits us, we'll either carry it around as an insecurity or we'll panic and try to stick it on someone else. Just one judgmental thought, one piece of gossip, that we overhear in childhood can, over time, cause us shame, anxiety, and eventually lead us to feeling suicidal or violent. It all starts and ends with one, little, hateful thought. It does not even have to be directed at anyone in particular. It could be about "people" or "women" or "men." To be harmful, it needs only to deny our inner potential, equality, and connection. It needs only to speak of good and bad, of those who deserve love and those who don't.

177

When you see a person acting violently, ask yourself whether he knows how powerful he is. If he knew his power, would he feel the need to assert it? Does he know that he is eternal, immortal, and indestructible? Or, does he think that he is a temporary body that is defined by its superiority to other bodies? Just like a person full of fear equates courage with death or a person with wounds equates vulnerability with death, the violent person equates weakness with death. He does not know that he is already strong, without needing to prove or earn it. He thinks that his value depends solely on his ability to prove himself better than others. Some people learn this directly from the teachings of a love-hungry relative, while others learn this deductively by running out of options. These teachings spread virally from person to person, none of them ever knowing their true essence. Without any hope for safety or certainty, sometimes the only option a person sees is to harm others. The violent person, the one we call villain, perceives no choice.

Mindset controls experience. Villain thoughts, not any innate downfalls or inadequacies, are precisely what control aggressive and passive aggressive people. Take the abusive spouse. Hateful thoughts fill her head when she looks at her partner. They stew, build, and rule her mind. These thoughts completely control her emotions. Though she may try, she cannot keep these emotions in for long. She explodes. Afterwards, she tells him she will do better, and she really tries. She tries not to act on her emotions. Again, she fails because she tries to augment the wrong part of the equation. She goes after the abusive behaviours instead of the real culprits: the abusive thoughts.

Some villain thoughts have reached frightening proportions. During times of war, political figures often spread propaganda about the enemy. Hundreds and thousands of people march indignantly, ready to kill, maim, and torture all because of the judgmental thoughts fed to them every day. In some cults, children begin to get indoctrinated with villain thoughts on the same day they start walking. By the time they reach adolescence, they'll gladly take a gun or strap a bomb to themselves in the name of acting against the villain. Then, we watch them with their guns and bombs, and we call *them* villains. Round and round we go.

The so-called villains do not pop out of the womb as villains. They ride on the downward spiral. Their minds receive hateful thoughts until, eventually, their roots have soaked up so much poison that the leaves turn brown. Even when they are shown kindness, they find it difficult—if not impossible—to receive. Villain thoughts are blocks to receiving love. The less we love others, the less we can allow ourselves to be loved. The less we allow ourselves to be loved, the less people try. This sort of spiral takes place in thousands of people every single day. It happened to every school shooter and every serial murderer. Of course, the stories differ, but the origin is the same—love deprivation lies at the core of each story of violence.

Often, people speak of human nature as being good or bad. In truth, there is no good or bad in human nature, just like there is no good or bad in a tree's nature. Our nature is simply to love and be loved. When we follow our nature, we tend to be "good" in the same way that a thriving tree is "good." The healthy tree cleans the air and the healthy human cleans the world. There is no good or evil, only hunger and health.

*

The greatest illusion that perpetuates our making villains out of one another is the idea that, if we love people who do bad things, we approve of those bad things. If we forgive those who have hurt us, we tell them that it is acceptable to hurt us again. If we extend compassion to the killers, rapists, and bombers, then we condone those deeds. If we love those who insult, beat, or threaten us, we make ourselves their prey. Loving a villain seems to be an act of weakness, resignation, and submission. This attitude keeps people from loving one another and, by natural consequence, from loving themselves.

"Not forgiving," says author Anne Lamott, "is like drinking rat poison and then waiting for the rat to die." Withholding love from the villain is an act of violence against the self. We cannot opt out of love awareness selectively. Either we accept our deepest truth or we don't. Either we love everyone or we don't love anyone. If we hold a grudge against just one person, we cannot receive love. Hateful thoughts are certain to change one person—the thinker, and that change is never positive. We must forgive. We must love. To forgive is to understand the past, not excuse it. To accept that something has happened and that it happened for a reason—this gives us true freedom, not only from the effects of hate on our minds, but from accidentally perpetuating hateful, abusive cycles in the future out of the misunderstanding that someone hurt us simply because they were "bad" and we just need to find someone "good."

In my experience, the actual practice of loving the villain becomes exponentially easier over time. This sort of thinking is most difficult in the beginning. Often, the healing person will have a storage house of painful memories and triggering images connected to the villain. To think compassionate, accepting thoughts towards her can be difficult and unnatural at first. However, as we feed ourselves loving thoughts, and as these thoughts turn into a loving mindset, understanding flourishes. We open up more and more each time we allow ourselves to practice awareness. Then, we begin to see the villain as a helpless child, as a victim, as a product of her environment. We see the path of events that has led her here and, suddenly, it is perfectly understandable why she hurt us. After all, she was in so much pain; she was so hungry for love. Having reached this understanding, we can forgive completely and wholeheartedly.

Often the greatest leap of understanding happens in a time of action. To act kindly towards a person previously perceived as a villain usually requires some mindset development beforehand. You must, by way of loving thoughts, open your mind so that love can begin to flow where it once stopped short. Then, you can act. You can stand in front of your villain and see him for the beautiful, powerful soul underneath his hungry, unaware exterior. You can see beyond the damaged, external body deep into the core. In that state, you will not resist his actions or words, and neither will you submit to them. You will simply accept them. You will accept his words, emotions, and actions like you'd accept them in someone who's just broken her arm. You will allow pain and suffering to take its natural form in that place and time, just like you would allow a sick child to vomit. Thus, you will find yourself across from a person who is shocked, confused, perhaps immobile. Unable to push you away or push you down, the villain will stop struggling. Each villain has a breaking point. This is when the external self stops violently resisting, because the mind, for a moment, detects the nourishment of the soul. You may just trigger the villain's love-deprived mind into love awareness.

There, you will see a helpless, hungry person. There will be a person who is not so menacing and not so evil. There will be someone who needs love more than, perhaps, anyone else you've ever encountered. There will be someone who is just like you.

Such moments of understanding can, of course, occur in your head. You can realize this about your former villains and find strong love for them. In practice, however, is the only way that you will directly experience the villain's unfamiliarity with the act of unconditional love. It is in such a moment that the villain's motivations become clear. He does not love because he does not know what love is. No one has ever shown him. We can know this in theory, but it becomes crystal clear in practice. It is only once you see the baffled expression on the face of your enemy when you give his cruel words a warm smile that you'll understand, truly understand, what love is all about. Of course, the breaking point of the villain's violent resistance may lie far beyond what you are able to (or should ever have to) withstand. There is a gentle, woven balance between the mental practice of love awareness and acting on that awareness—a balance we must all discover for ourselves.

What if we were to err on the side of love, instead of always erring on the side of fear, judgment, and apathy? We live in a society of people seeking therapy because therapists are accepting. They do not react with offence or resentment to the client's words. They simply nod; they accept and allow. In such a space, even the most heavily hooded villain can take off her robes and expose the wounds hidden under all that armour. In our love-hungry society, those who are willing to reach out for support have some hope, while those who are unwilling to ask for help are doomed to suffer in silence or externalize their pain onto others. What if the way we learned to interact with one another could change that?

What if we saw potential within the villain to heal, to grow, to contribute? What if we recognized the villain as a real person to whose suffering we are all vulnerable? Until we can learn to see beyond our judgments of hero and villain, abusive and sweet, angry and calm, good and bad—we will see only mirages of human beings. Within, we are all beautiful and eternal. We all have the same nature. We are made to come together, to unite, to love. We thrive on it. When we deny this nature, it is through ignorance, not intent. When we can see our own self, angry and hurting others, within every villain, then we can love. When we can see our own desperate struggle for belonging in the eyes of every enemy, then we can love. When we can look at the greatest of atrocities and see the opportunity for healing within, then, and only then, can we really love.

13

THE PREACHER AND THE TEACHER

*The greatest enemy of knowledge is not ignorance, it is the
illusion of knowledge.*

STEVEN HAWKING

Coming closer to the end of our journey, if you have
not already, then you will soon begin to see within
yourself the seeds of a teacher. If what you are
learning about love is helping to relieve your suffering and unearth your potential, then the ideas
within this book have likely made a home inside
your mind. Perhaps you have begun to look at
yourself and others in a different light. Perhaps you

have opened yourself to receive the warmth of love and felt its healing, nourishing energy. Here, you find yourself in a place that feels like the end of the journey. It may seem that, now, what you must do is to spread the message of this wonderful thing called love into the farthest corners of the earth. Here, you are at a critical point in the learning process. It is a fork in the road. On one side, you go down the path of being a teacher and, on the other, that of a preacher.

When we first come upon something new and inspiring, it takes hold of our awareness. Some little idea, like any other thought, can grow into an obsession within just a few weeks. This sort of selective, overwhelming passion is familiar to most of us. This is the process we've taken with lovers, songs, and hobbies. It starts with one innocent exposure that triggers some pleasant feeling within us. Then, we crave to have the feeling again. The mind does its algorithm and answers the heart's pining. It tells us to return to whatever gave us the pleasant feeling in the first place. Like this, we breed romantic obsession. Like this, we fall for fads. Like this, we become infatuated with ideas. Like this, I first fell for love. The idea of love, ironically enough, became a trigger for the experience of it.

Just like any obsessed lover, she who is obsessed with an idea wants to climb up on the rooftops and shout its name. From her higher ground, she seeks to teach, yet ends up preaching instead. The thoughts that have inspired her have only just begun to make their home inside her mind. The thoughts have triggered the feelings, perhaps repeatedly so, but they have not solidified into a mindset and have not produced any lasting change in her actions. Thus, from the rooftops shout the preachers who are all theory without practice, all thought without action.

There, on that rooftop, is a dangerous place. It is neither here nor there. You are no longer ignorant, yet you do not fully know. This place is much more harmful than ignorance, because it breeds condescension, judgment, and stagnation. Reading about villains, you may first notice the villains in your own mind, yet without further mind training, the natural course of your thoughts will be to start identifying instances of villain thoughts in everyone around you. Then, it is no longer about you and *your* villain thoughts; it becomes about others and *their* villain thoughts. Such externalization of concepts is, in all cases, a way to prevent action. It happens to the so-called villains, those who observe the villains, and those who observe those who observe the villains. The tendency to preach—to speak theory without corollary action—is the most famous and dangerous way to keep from real change.

*

To wake up to the truth of love and the truth of your identity in Western culture is, undoubtedly, shocking. At first, it feels like walking around in public completely naked. It is frightening to have all your elements of self-identification stripped away along with all your misconceptions about relationships. Stripped to the core, you float in space, no longer attached gravitationally to everything that you used to feel was important. Though thoughts of immortality, power, and eternity feel like fresh water on the roots of your mind, most people around you have never received this water. Most people in our culture have been soaking up acid rain since the day they were born.

Around our orchard full of living trees are various polluting factories. They are the factories of media, government, and commercialism. They are factories of tradition, education, and culture. These factories pollute the air around us and block the sun. Not only do they block one source of sustenance, they taint another. When it rains, because of all the pollution around us, it is acid rain. Our roots soak up toxic chemicals. If a tree in the forest was exposed to these chemicals, it would surely die. We, however, are more resilient. Our orchard has been here for a while and we, as a whole collective, have acclimatized to the chemicals in the water. We still grow tall and our roots still burrow deep. We may be warped, mutated, and unhealthy, but we're just as tall as any other tree. To realize, suddenly, that this is not the best way to live, is shocking. The mutated tree that finds itself in an orchard surrounded by other mutated trees may become aware of its present situation, but it will have great difficulty formulating any plan of future action.

The shock of realizing the truth in the midst of living out a lie puts us in an interesting place. It is a place that demands action. Having realized that I'm capable of so much more than I am doing, what will I choose to do? Will I take personal responsibility for getting myself out of this situation? Will I try to change this situation? Will I find someone to blame for my misfortune? Intuitively, I know that I should take responsibility and change. I try and I find that change isn't as easy as I thought. I feel lost, uncertain, and confused. How can I get myself out of here? How can I put this into practice? Here I am, in this polluted air, soaking up this acid rain. I don't know what to do. I feel helpless. I cannot, however, do nothing. Just like a love-hungry person will gossip to take the pressure off her own self-loathing, the awakening person will preach to take the pressure off his helpless, desperate desire for change.

Here is where we get our preachers. These are the people who tell us what to think and feel, what to do and say, without actually practicing it. If we need help, if we want the truth, we instinctively mistrust the preachers. We would not take weight loss advice from an overweight person and we would not take advice about truth from someone who continues to live within the lie. The preacher believes that he is saving people. He thinks he is sharing with them the seeds of wisdom that he has acquired. He believes he is helping. What he is really doing, however, is stalling. He talks about change in order to avoid it. He speaks of the truth because he does not know how to live the truth. Then, he comes to the next stage.

There is only so long that we can spend talking and talking, while our roots receive nothing but acid rain day in and day out. Eventually, the preacher is bound to grow frustrated. Then, he begins to project his emotions as well. He is dissatisfied with the giant love-sized hole within him. The blame for this dissatisfaction then befalls the listeners who are not attending, not acting, not changing. The preacher shakes his head at those who listen to him, telling them that they should know better. He warps his pronouns, but he knows, deep inside, that it is he who already knows better. Knowledge without action puts the preacher into an extremely painful place—a place where he cannot simply live out the lie like everyone else. In the absence of action, he begins to rationalize, warp, and distort what he once knew to be the truth. Here is where most preachers find themselves. Here is the stagnant, poisonous ground on which many religions continue to thrive.

Trees that soak up acid rain inevitably grow mutated or die. They become what they are fed. No matter how much we fight it, this continues to be true. Likewise, people will only perform and perceive within the confines of their mental nourishment. People's minds can only be as healthy as the thoughts they have been fed. This is not to say that we do not have a personal responsibility to seek the truth, to seek what is good for us. This is merely to say that every external form is an accurate representation of its nourishment. We become what we're fed. Everyone is simply doing the best that they can with the resources they have available. Inside of all of us, there is an inner core with the same boundless wealth of potential as everyone else. In order to make use of this potential, however, we must first see it as a resource. We do not use resources that we do not know we have. Thus, everyone is just functioning at their peak within their own level of awareness.

What happens when we feed on some truth that does not match our external environment is that we, like our preacher, get introduced to a new level of awareness, a new consciousness. Realizing that we are capable of doing more than we are doing is extremely painful, because this means we are no longer performing at the peak of our perceived potential. We naturally develop the drive to take that pain away. The most immediate way is to share that pain with others, to spread the awareness. This quick fix, like most quick fixes, does not help. If anything, it breeds misery. What if you do manage to wake up others in the acid rain orchard to the reality of their plight? Then, your misery has company. Then, you are no longer in limbo alone — you have others with you. This is how we get groups of angry, militant activists. These are people who know that something is wrong, but they continue to live within it. They know something better is possible, but they focus all their energy on protesting what exists and not on creating what can be.

Ironically, some of the cruellest people are those who are further down the path towards love awareness. Some of the most judgmental people are those who are on the right track towards non-judgment. When we stop halfway through a process, we are worse off than those who never start. If we have eaten nothing but scraps for an entire lifetime, we can be effortlessly grateful. We do not know anything else is possible. Suppose, however, that you spend your days eating out of garbage cans and someone gives you a mouth-watering, twelve course feast. Then, you are in pain. You can no longer live under the delusion that scraps are all that exist. With the first scraps of knowledge, the first thoughts, comes the erasure of ignorance. With that, if we do not persist in developing our mindset, we continue to suffer. Simply knowing the truth will never be enough—we must act on it.

*

I remember once speaking to a family member about judgment. We were standing in an elevator as the ding of each passing floor echoed softly off the mirrored walls. I had said something about the idea of withholding judgment. My words, I do not remember clearly, but I remember her reply like it was yesterday. "That doesn't sound right," she said. "If I don't tell people when they are wrong, how can I make them change?"

This question, I realized, lives within the mind of every preacher. I have been guilty of this thinking many times in my life. Each epiphany brings with it the narcotic hum of delaying action by preaching, and historically, I have succumbed to it more times than I have not. Behind each lecture and sermon has been a compulsive need to act, to change, to transform. The road to hell, as they say, is paved with good intentions.

How, then, do we change the world, change people? How do we go from preacher to teacher? Despite what some may say, it *is* possible to change people. However, this is not something that we can do directly. Just like you cannot feel an emotion by forcing it, you cannot change people by forcing them. If our emotions are like the fruits on a tree, our ability to change the world is the seeds. Once the tree is healthy, the seeds will spread.

The mistake the preacher makes is thinking that she should stay in the poisoned orchard. She thinks that her seeds will be healthy, because she has an idea of what produces healthy seeds. All the while, the factories keep polluting. The first thing the preacher must do is to give up delaying—to stop telling others about the factories, the acid rain, the pollution. Next, she must do the thing that is so simple, yet it is rarely easy. She must uproot herself and go where there is no pollution.

If you think back to teachers you have respected, you will see that they practice what they preach. We all have an inner intuition for authenticity, for matched up internal and external truth.

When we detect this, we feel immediate comfort. We know truth when we hear it. Thus, the preacher calls for our attention, while the teacher already has it. The preacher fights each day against the acid rain, while the teacher has long since left an empty hole in the poisoned orchard. In a field with clean air and fresh rainwater, the teacher stands and, now, the students appear. All of the energy that a preacher expends on speaking, the teacher, first, expends on acting. Only then, the teacher speaks, but this speech does not come from pain avoidance. This speech comes from love. It falls like seeds and grows within the minds of those who are ready to change. Then, together, they can take on the polluting factories—strong and united.

The teacher, then, does not seek to be a teacher. The teacher primarily seeks to awaken and live the truth. The transformed person is a revolutionary only because he has revolutionized himself. He gives the people inspiration by holding up a mirror to their inner substance. We all know, intuitively, that if something is humanly possible, it is possible for ourselves. This is what a real teacher does: she opens the gates of our minds to the possibilities of our deepest potential.

14

THE CHALLENGE

To love for the sake of being loved is human, but to love for the sake of loving is angelic.

ALPHONSE DE LAMARTINE

You and I live in a world that does not understand the act of true love. Western society places romantic gestures on a fiery pedestal. The act of love is equivalent, in the average person's mind, with the act of passion. Love is giving you flowers. Love is telling you that you are beautiful. Love is climbing up a seventeen-floor fire escape to your window and professing my undying affection for you. Love is my inability to think of anything else except you.

Love is poetry, sex, and favours. Love is something we must make time for three times a week.

To know the truth about love is to know that love is, simultaneously, all of those things and none of them. Of course, such acts feel nice, but we are only enthralled because they are triggers. Book after book on relationships teaches us to learn to trigger one another better. Supposedly, if we can recognize those triggers in one another and fulfill them, there's a lifetime of love waiting. Such acts may trigger our love awareness, but they are not—and can never be—representations of love itself. In our eternal reality, those firework acts are nothing. They explode as fast as they fizzle.

In this way, our lives have become an inter-related web of transactions. I give you *this*, only so you will give me *that*. I'll tell you that you're strong if you tell me I'm beautiful. I'll spend time with you if you whisper me sweet nothings. I'll forgive you if you forgive me. I'll be nice if you'll be nice. I'll commit if you'll commit. As long as these transactions are balanced, our relationships with others run smoothly. As long as our kind and loving actions are met with applause, we'll keep doing them. However, the moment that our kind words meet anger or our acts of service receive ingratitude, we grow indignant, cold, and distant. Most people are only willing to give as much as they can get back. To do anything else brings forth images of selfless martyrdom reserved for those special people over there; those people who have nothing to do with me. I am a regular person and I just want to get what I deserve, to receive what I give, to be loved like I love.

Such a transactional view of relationships keeps us chained into constantly fluctuating cycles of self-love and self-loathing, romance and resentment, loving and losing. We continue to find ourselves empty-handed. When our triggers lose their power, we are broken-hearted and bare. We feel like we are starting over, beginning once again the race to find the most dependable trigger and to become such a trigger. This life of enslavement keeps us hungry and empty, isolated and helpless.

Out of these cycles stems the pervasive victim mentality of our age. Yes, I had those dreams so long ago, but because of this and that thing that you did, I had to give up. Of course, I have tried to be forgiving and compassionate to him, but he is cold, demeaning, and doesn't listen, so I can't do it anymore. When I first heard about changing my thoughts and taking responsibility for my life, I gave it my all, I really did, but my family didn't approve. I had to stop, you see, because they didn't love the new me that I tried to be. It's not my fault. It's their fault for not supporting my journey to find my authentic self. I'm still dying, but it is their doing, not mine.

In this part of the journey, you might desperately want to move into the mountains somewhere. Perhaps, you'll want to join some temple, monastery, or village of people who are all committed to love, peace, and healing. And perhaps, for a while, such a trip may serve you, inspire you, open you. But when you return, this broken world will be waiting for your loving arms to embrace it, having nothing tangible to give you in return. This is, perhaps, the greatest challenge of our time—to love in the absence of any immediate external rewards for our love.

*

While the movies would have you think otherwise, the act of love is rarely surrounded by swelling music and fireworks. It does not come with pretty

bows or in the midst of well-choreographed pro-
posals. Frequently, it is not even noticed. If it is, it's
often dismissed, ridiculed, or otherwise misunderstood. The act of love is often overlooked in the
name of more dazzling, important things. It is not
until many years later, and sometimes never at all,
that we look back on those acts that we so casually
ignored and see them for what they really were.
Sometimes we're the recipients and sometimes we
aren't. We see kindness and it may elude our
awareness in the moment, but when we awaken, we
remember.

In my bandages and armour, I was a black
hole for all compassion. In fact, I disdained it. Perhaps you know someone like this. Perhaps you are
someone like this. Each act of kindness seems to
have a hidden agenda. Each loving word or deed
strikes a chord of irritated entrapment. Receiving
kindness leads to thoughts like—are you just doing
this so I'll do it back for you? I don't have the time,
effort, or the willpower to do the same for you. Are
you manipulating me with all your so-called gener-
osity? What is the cost of this? What will I have to
give in return for what you've given me?

And thus, the love hungry person will disdain the loving action. He'll see it as an act of control. And, sometimes, it is one. The person who gives and gives to others, without taking any time or effort for herself, could be called manipulative. Of course, she does not do this purposefully, but behind her actions, there is a core principle: giving equals getting. She wants to receive so she keeps giving and giving, hoping that, one day, she'll get something back. When she doesn't, she feels like a victim. Then, those who don't give to such a victim feel pigeonholed and trapped. Like this, the "loving act" is warped by both the giver and the receiver.

We have been taught, by such occurrences, to mistrust kindness. Even when we give kindness, it is often with the intention of receiving something in return. Knowing this about ourselves makes us question it in others. We project our own self-service onto all others. And thus, the act of love is completely overlooked and lumped in with all self-serving acts. To extend compassion to a so-called villain, to forgive those who have wronged you, and to find common ground with someone who has been awfully isolated are not acts typically met with fireworks and swelling violins. More often than not, they are pushed away. To love, really love, is to do them anyway.

To allow oneself to be pushed away by the mistrustful recipient of kindness is to fulfil the recipient's prophecy. If your loving acts, receiving no reward, suddenly turn to self-victimization, then they were not loving acts in the first place. Just like the wary recipient thought, you had a hidden agenda. If we allow ourselves to wane in our love awareness due to a lack of external approval, then we cannot really say that we have love awareness. Love is always present and receiving it is always in our own hands, not in the hands of a circumstance or a response. Only love that continues to flow in times of anger, blame, and indifference can be called love. All else is simply a transaction. All else is temporary, fleeting, and bound to end.

Ironically, the reason that most of us don't give as abundantly as we can is because we limit what we receive while wait for a reward. We insist on being given love after we give it, instead of taking and giving freely. We make someone dinner and then we sit and starve until they come back with a dinner for us. The truth is—you don't need a reward for your kindness or compassion just like you don't need a reward for breathing. You breathe to live. You love to live. No one must congratulate you on breathing or approve of it. You simply know that it is the right thing to do and no one can ever convince you otherwise.

In this state, something funny happens. When you stop caring about what you get back from what you give, you create ripples of love all throughout every room you enter, every person you speak to, every place you go. For this, you may not get any credit. Maybe, you spend some time with a person and, a few days later, her anger wanes and she finds a new thirst for life. She does not know, necessarily, that this is because you gave her compassion. You may never know either. Because you do not focus on making every interaction into a transaction, you give and receive constantly, without keeping tabs.

With the love mindset, you spread joy simply by existing. And perhaps, years later, those people who received your kindness might just understand the value of what you've given them. Though your acts of love and compassion cannot penetrate bandages or armour, they are never wasted and never lost. They sit within the recipient's mind, awaiting his awakening. If he does awaken to love, he'll remember you. He'll remember what you said and did. The reward, then, may come years later, perhaps long after you pass on. And although acknowledgement may be nice, it will never be necessary. To spread the ripples of love is reward within itself.

*

To love regardless of consequence and simply for the sake of loving is not something reserved for spiritual deities or especially evolved people. It is not a privilege for those who do not need to slave for a living, nor a distant goal that, if you do all the correct rituals, you'll someday reach. Love awareness is now. Love is here, now. There is no need to become anything or earn it in some way. There is no need to struggle through levels of ascending awareness or consciousness, nor gain a certain amount of life experience before love can become your reality. There is no exam or qualification for this awareness, nor for acting out of it. People say things like "We can't all be Mother Teresa," and they leave it at that. They reserve unconditional, eternal love for people who are more "evolved." Like this, we live in an era of spiritual anorexia.

No living organism would deny itself the nourishment it requires on purpose. There is not a tree in the world that would deny fresh water to its roots or sunlight on its leaves. There is not a hungry bird that would refuse a worm nor a ravenous lion that would refuse meat. To do so would be to deny the rules of life by which all impermanent forms abide. We, however, are different because of our minds. We have not learned the truth of who we are, so we've taken on cultural conditioning as an authority. Anorexia is an epidemic of people starving themselves to match some outside, imposed norm of how they are supposed to look. Spiritual anorexia is an epidemic of people starving their souls in the name of conforming to some outside, imposed norm of what it means to be a human being. Saying that love is something reserved for special people is a form of self-denial. It is blindness at its finest. It is nourishment declined by a self-terminating mechanism.

You need love like you need food, air, and water. As does everyone else. The love that some call Mother Teresa love—the love that extends to all living beings—is not special. It is true. It is real. It is eternal. It is what we come from and what we need. Though Einstein invented the theory of relativity, it does not apply exclusively to him. Though Newton discovered the law of gravity, he is not the only one who abides by it. By the same token, those who have spread love and compassion into the world, though they have popularized the message, are not the only ones to whom those concepts apply. Love is universal, eternal, and, most certainly, for all of us.

When we think of unconditional love, we tend to picture selflessness. This is where we perceive pain. We think that, if we give without regard for what we get back, we'll get less than our fair share. Love, however, is not selfless at all. It is deeply selfish; it is perfectly in line with the authentic self. By serving humanity, I automatically serve myself. An act of love, then, is not an act for you rather than for me. It is an act for you as well as for me. Love is for us.

Love helps us all. When I love my enemy, it is a kindness to us both. It is a win-win situation. In love, there is no need to choose between self and other, because self *is* other. All that is true of me is true of you. If I act on the truth of who I really am, then I immediately act on the truth of who you really are. I am an advocate of the ever-present life that moves powerfully through every moment and I am not affected by something as feeble as approval or something as short-lived as rejection. I am what I am and I do what I do. I am love and I act out of love.

While we tend to think of love as some faraway place, it is actually a place nearby that we have forgotten. To love is to return home to your true self. There, it does not matter how others react to your transformed self or your ideas. Even if you are ostracized by those who loved your bandages and armour, your authentic self will keep shining. You know, in this place, that no matter how much love a mask receives, it is still a mask. Plaster does not absorb sunshine. To accept the truth of who you are is to become a lifelong, unconditional servant of love in all of your words and deeds. You need not act in the name of approval any longer. Only those who are suffering from love deprivation do that. Those who love, truly love, can be coerced into nothing.

Of course, with your newfound insight, you will need to return to your everyday life. The love mindset is not about selling all your possessions and becoming a robe-laden charity giver. It is not about moving into the mountains and chanting all day, nor dedicating your life to saving children from hunger—unless you want to, of course. This is a common fear people have of unconditional love. They believe that it comes with the burden of a hundred necessities. But to have a love mindset does not necessitate anything. It is simply a lens for reality. We can perceive reality through a clear lens or a soiled one. The love mindset gives you clarity. With such clarity, you do not need to obsess about making the right decisions. When you work on living from your inner truth, everything that is incompatible with your new understanding will eventually fall away. You will stop desiring poison and begin to desire healthy nourishment. This process will happen naturally. Of course, you will need to work hard to respond to your new understanding and your new desires, but there is a difference between working hard to create a life that truly serves you and working hard to create a life that you've been told you should want.

THE LOVE MINDSET

With your newfound awareness of yourself and others, you will make different choices. Over time, your bad habits and self-destructive patterns will lose their power, until you are no longer tempted to resort to them. You will laugh easier, and not need to take everything so seriously. You will help people around you, simply by understanding them. You will process through resentments of the past, against others and against yourself. You will become more comfortable with vulnerability, and thus be able to formulate relationships based on mutual acceptance and truth. You will shed your mask, like an onion, becoming more authentic with each year, each moment, each relationship. You will feel drawn to facing your fears, and you will experience self-confidence beyond your wildest dreams when you show yourself what you can do. You will find yourself desiring to contribute beyond yourself and give your abundant love to a world that desperately needs it. You will gain a sense of peace that permeates all of your emotions—you will not feel the need to extend pleasure or keep away pain. You will learn to fail and make mistakes. You will stop looking for a final answer, and realize that loving is a lifetime act. Like a tree on the cusp of death, love will first heal you, and then it will make you grow. In love, you will find the real meaning of happiness.

On your journey, you'll find that many people will think you strange, perhaps a fool. There's a certain childishness to living through love, because most children are more perceptive of our true nature than adults. It is a great irony that, when I lived through nothing but an old, tired story of my wounds, people thought me a genius. I was called strong, mature, intelligent. However, when I saw the truth and opened my heart to the love all around me, suddenly I was seen as immature, childish, weak, naïve. I feel my emotions without shame and I don't seem to grasp the evil in the world. Perhaps, then, there is nothing wrong with being childish. Perhaps naivety is simply the unwillingness to learn one's lesson. It is the decision to speak and live the truth, the beautiful truth of who we are and what we're capable of, against all odds and in the face of all opposition. If that is foolish, then call me a fool, for I'd rather be a fool in constant, unwavering love with myself and others than a lonely, miserable genius.

In my isolation, I dreamt of power. My daydreams and fantasies were all about how I could win, how I could be number one, how I could have my cake and eat it too. When those dreams were fulfilled, I felt nothing. The love-sized hole within me grew larger and larger as I died by my own hand, by my own mind. Then, I found what I needed to fill the hole. I found peace, joy, connection. To power, I waved goodbye. I thought that being a loving, spiritual being meant sacrificing that triumph-hungry drive within. For much too long, I ignored these urges, believing them to be the opposite of love while I cycled in and out of love awareness. The day that my love mindset became truly durable is when I realized that love is not the opposite of power. Love *is* power. Love is the strongest power there is. And, now, every time I watch a person awaken to their inner strength, I see what we're made of, and we're magnificent. We're brilliant. We really are. We crave magic because we *are* magic. We crave power because we *are* pure power.

Now, I still dream about power. I dream of the power of people who have realized the truth about themselves. I dream of a world full of courageous, resilient, evolved beings who respect their short stay on this planet and who seek to extract the most out of each relationship, each conversation, each moment. I dream of a world where outside circumstances cease to imprison us, because we have come to understand, really understand, the power of our minds. I dream of world peace, which is really inner peace within each individual mind. I dream of the power of love because, after all, the power of love is the power to change the world. And, really, who doesn't want to change the world? I know you do. So, live well and love well, my friend. I hope you make your short ride on this beautiful little planet worthwhile while you love with all your heart and, of course, all your mind.

GIVING THANKS

At times our own light goes out and is rekindled by a spark from another person. Each of us has cause to think with deep gratitude of those who have lighted the flame within us.

ALBERT SCHWEITZER

Perhaps the most important place to start is at the beginning. Though we usually tend to extend gratitude to those who have directly supported us, I think there is much to be said about being grateful for our struggles. I am eternally grateful to the people from my past who hurt me, though they certainly did not intend to. I am grateful for the opportunity to practice compassion towards others and myself, for the chance to overcome my struggles and become a healer. Without all the darkness, I doubt I would have been quite as intensely drawn to the light.

Next, I would like to thank my partner, Jamie, who has been my muse and my pillar, my greatest inspiration and my most treasured friend. Thank you for believing in me, encouraging me, and accepting me just the way I am. Thank you for being my greatest teacher about life, love, and happiness. You are my strength in times of weakness and my greatest joy in times of pride. You are a light in my life and a mirror that shows me the best in myself. I love you with all my heart.

This work also could not have been produced without the hard work and patience of my cover designer and friend, Nicole Williams, as well as my editor, Georgina Chong-You. Thank you Nikki, who has always been able to transform my words into images, my worries into comforts, and my lips into a smile. Thank you Georgina for treating my work with the same care with which you'd treat your own child. Thank you for helping me see what I couldn't.

I am also deeply grateful for my family. Thank you to my parents for bringing me into this world and teaching me the importance of hard work, perseverance, and courage. Thank you, mom, for crying and laughing when you read my writing back in elementary school. You showed me my potential to move people before I could see it myself. Thank you for believing in me and for teaching me, through your loyalty to your family in hard times, about unconditional love. Thank you, dad, for being the first who taught my mind to question, analyze, and explore the depths of the world around me. You were my first and most important teacher. Thank you to my aunt Marina for the light in your eyes when you spoke of this book before it even had a title. Thank you to my grandmother Zoya for always keeping me full of food and full of love.

I would also like to thank my friends who have supported me throughout the process with their ceaseless support, encouragement, and love. Thank you to Josh Kolic, Sarah Schulman, and Elsa Al-Attar for your big dreams for me and my contribution to the world. Thank you also to Theo Ignatieff, Alisha McLean, John Curtinhas, Ashley Martin, Nicole Alphonse, and Alanna Nish for being there with kind words and empathy, for believing in me, for being patient with me, and for seeing my potential. You knew me through my struggles and have seen me through my healing. Thank you for your faith, love, and support. I couldn't have done it without you.

Thank you also to my editor at Good Men Project, Justin Cascio, for seeing the beauty in my message of love and compassion before the world knew about it. Thank you to Matthew Melowany Forbes for encouraging me and for staying up all night reading my work. A special thank you to Jen Porter, who saw me through my darkest times and brightest times, who gave me kindness when I didn't think I deserved it, and who saw me beyond the façade.

Also a heartfelt thank you to everyone who has followed and spread my words. Your smiles, words, and engagement with my work are the lifeblood of my own ongoing spiritual journey. Thank you for seeing the wisdom and beauty of what I put forth, and for spreading it from the heart.

I am also eternally grateful for my teachers over the years. I tend to have intense whirlwind relationships with teachers and authors I've never met. Those I'm about to list have been such amazing contributors to my life. They have inspired me, moved me, and helped me become who I am. I am so eternally grateful for the guidance and teachings of: Marianne Williamson, Don Miguel Ruiz, Gangaji, Adyashanti, Deepak Chopra, Serge Kahili King, Neale Donald Walsh, Bob Proctor, Harriet Lerner, John Gottman, Sue Johnson, Wayne Dyer, Thich Nhat Hanh, Robert Prisig, Eckhart Tolle, and Byron Katie.

I'd also like to shine a special spotlight on two such teachers. Firstly, Brené Brown, who first opened me up to the idea of sharing my story. She showed me the power of authenticity and inspired me to dare greatly, be myself, and connect to others through the power of empathy. Thank you, Brené. Second, I'd like to thank Tony Robbins. You walked with me on every side street, sat with me in every coffee shop, and spoke to me through every conflict. You've become a part of me. You have been my teacher and my friend. I am eternally grateful for your work and the amazing effect that it's had on my life. You showed me what it looks like to really believe that people can change.

Finally, I'd like to thank all of the influential love teachers of the past who have paved the awareness of humankind for centuries. From Jesus to Lao Tzu, Martin Luther King to the Buddha, these courageous and enlightened leaders have continued to remind us of ourselves, to help us remember that we are eternal, beautiful, and capable of so much. Thank you to those who continue to show people the truth of who they are today and those who will continue to take on this valiant task in the future. With each person who finds inner peace and seeks to spread that message to the world, we all come closer to a world of unwavering peace, exuberant joy, and unconditional love.

COME FIND YOUR TRIBE

On your journey of self-discovery and healing, there is nothing like a supportive community of people who are on the same path. That's what the Love Tribes are all about.

A Love Tribe is a collection of people who come together to heal, grow, and change the world. It is a community based on love first. A Love Tribe is a support group for being human, a place where you can form a new family—a community willing to cheer you on when you're being brave, lift you up when you're down, and believe in you when you don't believe in yourself.

To read more and join, visit:

www.vironika.org/love-tribes

ABOUT THE AUTHOR

Vironika Tugaleva is a life coach, award-winning author, and inspirational speaker. Her work helps people cultivate self-love, heal mental and emotional suffering, develop healthy self-care habits, build deeper relationships with others, and unleash their inner potential to change the world.

Vironika is a different kind of teacher for a new generation. She doesn't wear makeup on her face and doesn't cover up her humanity. She openly speaks about her failures, imperfections, and struggles. She believes in being a guide, not a guru. She helps people become the experts on themselves.

For more from Vironika, please visit her website at www.vironika.org.